Early Man in West Middlesex

The principal author of this book, Desmond Collins, is Senior Lecturer in Prehistory at the University of London Department of Extra-Mural Studies. He has written numerous articles on Early Man and related subjects, at both academic and popular levels, and his most recent work, a full-length book, is *The Human Revolution*, published by Phaidon Press in 1976.

Desmond Collins, who is 37, was educated at Merchant Taylors School, Northwood, and at Gonville and Caius College, Cambridge, where he obtained an Honours Degree in the Tripos of the Faculty of Archaeology and Anthropology. He has since held several academic positions, and was from 1963 to 1973 Tutor for the University of Oxford Delegacy for Extra-Mural Studies. He has also participated in many excavations in the UK and abroad, some of which he directed, including the Mousterian period excavations at Oldbury rock shelters in Kent, and the Lower Palaeolithic excavations at Yiewsley.

Desmond Collins has been assisted by two contributors to this book, Tom Allen and Richard Hubbard.

Tom Allen, 42, is an authority on Pleistocene studies. For some years he studied under Professor S W Wooldridge, the pioneer of modern geomorphological research in the South-East area of Britain. For ten years he has been working on mapping and interpreting the Thames terraces. He is a member of the Quaternary Research Association.

Richard Hubbard, who is 32, was educated at Westminster and at Christ Church, Oxford where he graduated in chemistry. He went on to obtain his M Sc at London University's Institute of Archaeology where he is now completing his doctoral research at the Department of Environmental Archaeology, specializing in pollen, seeds and other vegetation remains from archaeological sites in Europe and West Asia.

Cover illustration

Early hunters in the Thames valley

Illustration: Allard Graphic Arts

Early Man in West Middlesex

The Yiewsley Palaeolithic sites

Desmond Collins
with contributions from
T J Allen and R N L B Hubbard

London   Her Majesty's Stationery Office

To Kenneth Oakley
whose work and friendship
have been a source of
great inspiration

ACKNOWLEDGEMENTS

In addition to the colleagues who have kindly
contributed papers, I would like to mention some
others who have been instrumental in this
publication. John Hayes, Director of the London
Museum, and his successor, Brian Spencer, made the
work possible. Roy Canham, the museum's Field
Officer, and Alison Laws, his assistant, helped and
encouraged us at all stages, especially in the excavations. They also provided facilities for Gordon King
who drew most of the tools and sections as well as
helping in the field. The assistance of all those who
contributed to the cleaning and drawing of sections
is much appreciated, while Barry Gray is to be
thanked for his splendid photographs. I am most
grateful to Philippa Glanville, Sally Kington and
David Challis for numerous editorial discussions. The
help of the staff of the British Museum Quaternary
Room is respectfully acknowledged, as is that of all
other custodians of collections examined. Professor
F Kenneth Hare and the Editor of the *Proceedings of
the Geologists' Association* kindly gave permission for
the reproduction of figure 4.

We owe a massive debt of gratitude to Messrs
Sabey and Company. They were most generous with
information and lent us some invaluable air photos
of the pits. It was through the good offices of their
Director, Mr P W G Penfold, that we borrowed a
drag-line to help clear the long sections and Mr D
Williams, the pit manager, and his men were
unfailingly helpful.

NOTES

All maps referred to are Ordnance Survey maps.

National Grid references are used throughout.

Lengths are given in metres. Heights are generally
given in feet above Ordnance Datum, with metric
equivalents.

CONTENTS

INTRODUCTION

The Yiewsley sites and the main points to arise from their investigation

The Palaeolithic material considered in this report comes from a series of pits, mostly commercial gravel workings, collectively known as Yiewsley in West Middlesex (figures 2 and 3). They lie close together, west of the Dawley Road and east of the 100 ft contour beside the Colne valley (figure 9). Pits extend 1 km south of the Grand Union Canal and 1 km north of it where the most northerly relevant one now being worked reaches as far as Gouldsgreen. The following are some of our principal conclusions.

Two gravel terraces rest on the London clay in the Yiewsley area at about 120 ft (about 36 m) OD and at 90 ft (27 m) OD. Their surfaces have been traced over a considerable area and they have been named the Stoke Park terrace and the Lynch Hill terrace. The latter contains the pits in which most of the Palaeolithic finds have been made.

Archaeologically the richest pit is that formerly called 'Eastwood's' (believed to be near TQ 078 800; figure 9); next comes 'Boyer's pit' some 500 m south-west, and 'Maynard's pit' some 500 m east. Some of these pits may well have been contiguous, but the practice of assigning them to different localities, for instance of referring to Maynard's pit as being in Dawley and Boyer's pit in West Drayton, has obscured the fact that they are close together in the same stretch of gravels. R G Rice, the principal collector of artefacts, whose bequest to the London Museum is considered in detail here, initiated the practice of referring to the whole area as Yiewsley.

Most of the Yiewsley Palaeolithic finds were made between 1885 and 1935. Today digging continues only in the northern part of the area, mainly in the higher terrace. Because of this, and present-day mechanical digging techniques, few artefacts are now found.

But the Yiewsley pits have yielded one of the largest series of Lower Palaeolithic stone tools in Europe and the area remains one of the richest Palaeolithic sites in Britain. According to data taken from the *CBA Gazetteer* (table 1), to explore different ways of measuring richness, Swanscombe comes out on top whichever index of classification is used but Yiewsley is second in a count of handaxes, and third in the other two relevant counts, of Levallois flakes and cores, and of artefacts as a whole. Some lesser-known collections were inevitably missed in the compilation of the *Gazetteer*, rendering totals somewhat low in most cases, but, comparing like with like, the *CBA* figures are a usually sound guide to relative richness.

The figures may in part simply show which sites have been excavated or intensely explored; though this is not the reason why Yiewsley comes out so high on all counts. Again, they may reflect only the size of the site within which recovery has been possible, but this would not favour the Yiewsley sites either, for they are not particularly large. Perhaps we may reasonably conclude that the sites which come near the top of the 'richness league' were not merely fleetingly occupied in the Palaeolithic, but were sites of prolonged, though not necessarily continuous, occupation.

FIGURE I
Aerial photograph of the Yiewsley pits in 1973. Warren Lake is clearly visible in the centre of the photograph. Figure 9 shows the location of the pits mentioned in the text and figure 7a shows the position of the long section drawn in 1972, at the east (right hand) end of the lake
Aerial photograph by Fairey Surveys Ltd

TABLE I Order of richness of Palaeolithic sites[1] according to four criteria

Class of artefact	Palaeolithic sites			
Handaxes	Swanscombe 3500	Yiewsley[3] 2190	Warren Hill 2000	Broom 1827
Levallois flakes and cores	Swanscombe[2] 1540	Acton 747	Yiewsley 455	New Hythe 296
Tools including Levallois flakes and handaxes	Swanscombe 5500	Yiewsley 2645	Warren Hill 2000	Broom 1830
Artefacts including waste flakes	Swanscombe 20 000	Caddington 4140	Yiewsley 3943	Purfleet 3840

1 Data from Derek A Roe. 1968. A gazetteer of British Lower and Middle Palaeolithic sites. *CBA Research Report*, 8.

2 Including Northfleet.

3 As a postscript to the *CBA* figures for Yiewsley, we should add 6 handaxes found recently in the Warren Lake area (now in West Drayton Library and in Sabey's Stockley works office). The Sadler collection in Gunnersbury House Museum also has 6 handaxes, 5 Levallois and 3 other flakes. There are a number of private collections unaccounted for; for example, the writer has in his teaching collection 13 handaxes from Yiewsley, given by G F Cole in 1958, found in about 1930, together with 4 flakes and a tortoise core.

Meanwhile, tool totals in hundreds or even thousands, as they are at Yiewsley, give a reliable picture of the complete range of types in a way which is impossible for those sites yielding only a few artefacts.

There has been little research into the Yiewsley area, or even the British Lower Palaeolithic in general, until recently. But the last few years have seen a revival of interest in this field and, in particular, pollen analysis has been applied to a number of sites. The discovery of pollen in both terraces and in altogether four different strata at Yiewsley has been a landmark. The terraces contain no fossil bones or shells and until now it has been thought that any correlation based on fossil content would be impossible and that palaeobotanical work on river gravels and loams was futile. In fact both terraces contain the pollen of trees including warmth-loving types such as oak.

The archaeological and geological sequences at Yiewsley parallel those at Swanscombe in many respects and as many as five different archaeological stages are shared by the two sites, a number unique in our knowledge of Europe at such a remote period. The main occupations at Swanscombe and Yiewsley are dated to the last but one interglacial complex, some 200000–250000 years ago, and to the immediately following glacial period.

A feature unique to Yiewsley is the presence in a higher level of stone tools of a Middle Palaeolithic (Mousterian) date, isolated here for the first time, and indicating occupation during the Neanderthal period some 70000 years ago – a period of man's development otherwise poorly represented in the archaeology of Britain.

These papers were finished at the end of 1973 and have not been rewritten to take account of more recent developments.

Desmond Collins

FIGURE 2
Map of the Thames
valley showing places
mentioned in the text.
The area of figure 3 is
highlighted

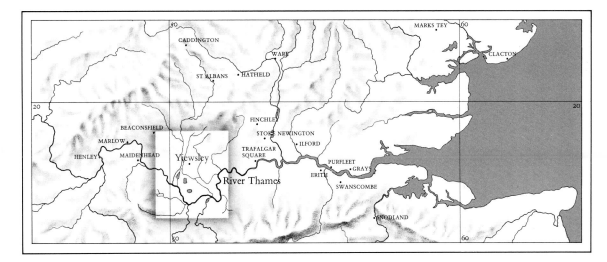

FIGURE 3
Map of the environs of
Yiewsley, with the
location of the pits as
shown in figure 9

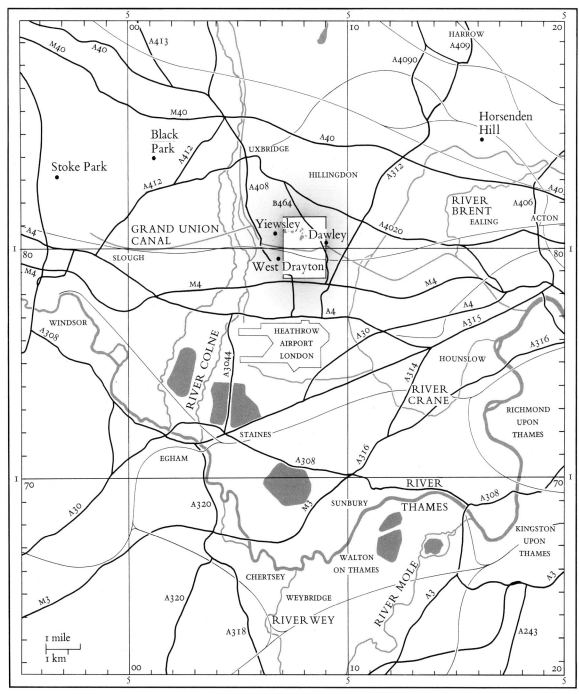

On all maps grid lines
are those of the
Ordnance Survey
National Grid

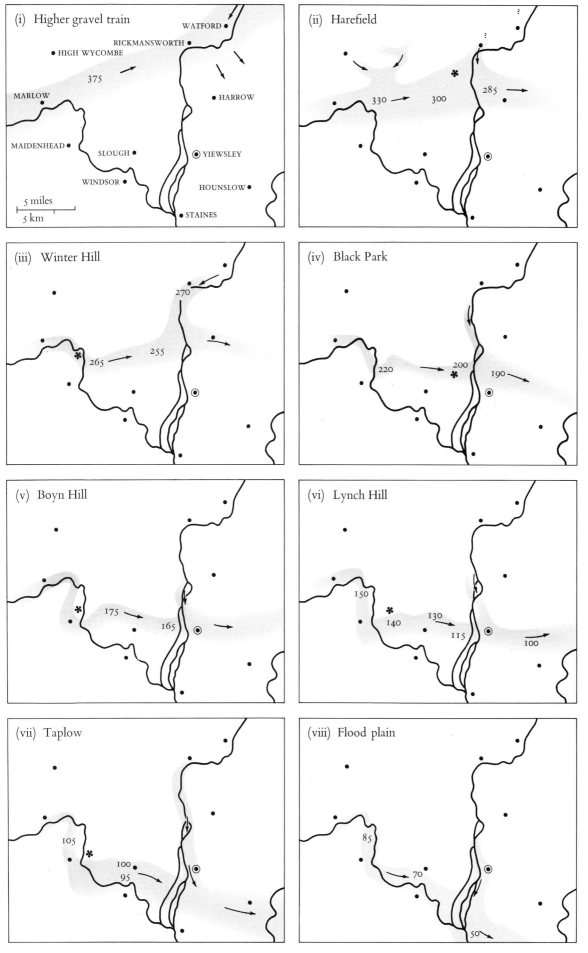

(i) Higher gravel train

WATFORD
RICKMANSWORTH
HIGH WYCOMBE
375
MARLOW
HARROW
MAIDENHEAD
SLOUGH
YIEWSLEY
WINDSOR
HOUNSLOW
STAINES
5 miles
5 km

(ii) Harefield

?
?
*
330   300   285

(iii) Winter Hill

270
*
265   255

(iv) Black Park

220   200   190

(v) Boyn Hill

*
175   165

(vi) Lynch Hill

150
*
140   130
115
100

(vii) Taplow

105
*
100
95

(viii) Flood plain

85
70
50

FIGURE 4
Stages in the development of the Thames. Redrawn from Hare (1947), figure 34; Palaeogeography of the eight main stages in the development of the modern drainage system.

Arrows indicate the direction of flow of the river.

Figures indicate the height of the terrace in feet.

Stars mark the locality from which each terrace takes its name.

CHAPTER ONE

Disposition of the terraces of the river Thames in the vicinity of Yiewsley

By T J Allen

Although some of the earliest finds of fossil Mammalia and Lower Palaeolithic implements in the terraces of the river Thames took place in west London during the last century, investigation of the Pleistocene succession in this area has been overshadowed in recent years by examination of the terraces of the middle Thames west of the river Colne and of the lower Thames downstream from London. Yet the Pleistocene sequence within this intervening section of the river, the eastern part of the middle Thames between the rivers Colne and Brent, can command considerable interest. In this short stretch of river the long-profiles of the middle Thames terraces gradually come to assume the horizontal aspect characteristic of the eustatic terraces of the lower Thames (Pocock, 1903; Zeuner, 1945). Consequently, the extension into this area of the terrace mapping carried out in the middle Thames west of the Colne by F K Hare (1947), K R Sealy and Catherine E Sealy (1956) and M F Thomas (1961) constitutes an essential preliminary step towards relating the complex terrace succession found by these workers in the western and central sections of the middle Thames to the equally complex terrace record which has been mapped along the lower Thames east of the river Lea (Allen, unpublished), and in addition provides a necessary basis for further studies of local geology, geography and archaeology. The writer is currently engaged in mapping the terraces of the Thames in the vicinity of London from Staines downstream as far as the junction with the river Lea. A more comprehensive study of the terrace morphology of the section of the river between Staines and Swanscombe will be published when this project has been completed.

This chapter is limited to a discussion of the relationship between the terrace sequence of the Beaconsfield block and the eastern part of the middle Thames in order to place the archaeological and palynological studies presented in this volume in their context within the middle Thames terrace succession. A brief review of the history of previous research on the middle Thames terraces is followed by a description of the areal extent of each terrace within the eastern part of the middle Thames. The geology and archaeology of the terrace deposits in this area are discussed by Desmond Collins below, with special reference to a recent section in Sabey's pits at Yiewsley (TQ080 805). This section exposed deposits at the rear of the

Lynch Hill terrace and in the bluff of a higher terrace, mapped as being within the Boyn Hill gravels by the Geological Survey but clearly lying at a lower level than the Boyn Hill terrace as defined by Hare (1947). The preliminary results of an investigation by R N L B Hubbard into the palynology of the section are given in chapter 3, and a study by Peter Allen of the sedimentology of its deposits is currently in progress.

Previous research on the terraces of the middle Thames west of the river Colne

Separate terraces were not distinguished within the superficial deposits bordering the Thames when the drift cover was added to the one-inch old series geological maps of the middle and lower Thames in the years after 1861. In writing his notable memoir, *The geology of London and of part of the Thames valley* (1889), W Whitaker had no choice other than to treat the 'River Drift' as a single unit, though occasionally he used the terms 'high terrace', 'middle terrace' and 'low terrace' in his regional discussion of these deposits, and even presented a map of all three terraces in the vicinity of Maidenhead (Whitaker, 1889, figure 69). These three terraces were not mapped as separate units elsewhere in the Thames valley until the re-survey of its drift deposits on the six-inch scale by J A Howe and T I Pocock at the beginning of this century (Pocock, 1903). During the same period the researches of M A C Hinton and A S Kennard (1906) along the lower Thames, particularly in the vicinity of Grays and Swanscombe, enabled them to point out the presence of an additional '130 ft terrace' above the '100 ft' or 'High Terrace'. Four years later, Ll Treacher and H J Osborne White (1909) were able to demonstrate a similar duality of the 'High Terrace' at Maidenhead in the middle Thames. Soon after the commencement of six-inch field-mapping for the one-inch new series geological maps of the Thames valley doubts concerning the adequacy of the three-terrace system, and the realization of the dangers inherent in the application of the various schemes of altimetric and numerical terrace nomenclature adopted by workers along the lower Thames to the middle Thames, led C E N Bromehead (1912) to propose the use of local names for the river terraces on the one-inch sheets 255 (Beaconsfield) and 269 (Windsor). He suggested that 'the terms Boyn Hill Terraces and Taplow Terrace are convenient, the pits at both places being well-known, and identifiable even if future work should reveal higher or intermediate terraces' (Bromehead, 1912, 74). Succeeding years have shown the wisdom of these remarks. Geomorphological research has indeed greatly increased the number of terms in the terrace record of the middle Thames through the recognition of both higher and intermediate terraces, while the abandonment of his intention to apply the terrace names only locally and the extension of their use to the lower Thames necessitated a premature correlation of the terraces in these two areas which has been the source of much subsequent confusion.

The presence of terraces within the glacial gravel lying at a higher level than the three mapped terraces of the Thames is implicit in much of the earlier literature concerning these deposits. As early as 1895, the researches of H J Osborne White (White, 1895, 28) had led him to state 'the Glacial Gravel is nothing more than an old deposit of the Thames' and later he stressed the terraced nature of these deposits in his description of the superficial drifts in the area around Henley (Jukes-Browne and White, 1908). As mapping for the one-inch new series geological sheets progressed downstream, the early course of the Thames was traced north-eastwards, firstly to Watford by R L Sherlock and A N Noble (1912), and then onwards as far as Ware by R L Sherlock (1924). Beyond Ware, Sherlock thought the river had turned northwards through a gap in the Chiltern escarpment towards the Wash before being diverted southwards to its present line by the advance of a Pleistocene ice sheet. Our current knowledge of the complex relationship between the high-level fluviatile gravels and the glacial drifts is due in large measure to the work of Professor S W Wooldridge, particularly during the two decades before World War II. In an an impressive synthesis of his investigations during this period Wooldridge (1938) divided the drift deposits of the London basin into three groups, later termed Stage I, Stage II and Stage III (Wooldridge and Linton, 1939), and showed the crucial part played by the two successive glaciations and the intervening gravel trains of Stage II in the evolution of the Thames drainage system. At the close of Stage I Wooldridge (1938) believed the course of the Thames lay along the line of the Vale of St Albans, but this route was blocked by an early ice sheet which deposited the Older Drift, later called the Chiltern Drift (Wooldridge and Linton, 1955), causing the river to loop southwards through the Finchley Depression before rejoining the former line near Ware during the period in which the higher and lower gravel trains were laid down. Subsequently a second glaciation, the Eastern Drift, closed this route by advancing across the mid-Essex depression into the southern part of the county and pushed an ice-lobe south-westwards along the Finchley Depression as far as Finchley, thus forcing the Thames at the time of the aggradation of the

Winter Hill terrace to find yet another outlet still further south. The Boyn Hill and lower terraces belonging to Stage III follow this third route past London to the sea.

In the middle Thames between Henley and Bourne End deposits of all three stages are confined within the present Thames valley and the terrace flight has been considerably dissected by later erosion. Further downstream the Stage II and Stage III deposits increasingly diverge, the former being aligned towards the Finchley Depression, the latter lying further south along the present course of the river. East of the Colne only the Stage III terrace deposits are well preserved, the Stage II deposits having been largely removed by erosion as the rivers Pinn, Crane and Brent and their tributaries have cut back into the plateau of south Hertfordshire. However, in the area between Bourne End and the Colne, the terrace record has been preserved with almost classical perfection and 'all the successive stages of down-cutting, base-levelling and drift-accumulation are conveniently displayed' (Wooldridge and Linton, 1939, 101). Detailed morphological mapping in this area, termed the Beaconsfield block in this chapter, enabled F K Hare (1947) to identify not only the Stage III terraces of C E N Bromehead (1912) and the divisions within the Stage II deposits recognized by S W Wooldridge (1938), but also two further units which he named the Black Park terrace and the Lynch Hill terrace. The existence of these additional units in the terrace succession was not entirely unexpected. Two years earlier F E Zeuner (1945) had proposed the division of the Winter Hill terrace, already acknowledged by Wooldridge (1938) to be composite, into an upper 'Finchley Leaf' and a lower 'Kingston Leaf', which appear to correspond in large measure to the Winter Hill terrace and Black Park terrace as defined by Hare (1947). The existence of two separate terraces within the Boyn Hill gravels, noted by Treacher and White as early as 1909, had been amply confirmed by later research. In the vicinity of Maidenhead W B Wright (1937) called the lower feature the 'Furze Platt Terrace', while at Iver K P Oakley (King and Oakley, 1936) had recognized an 'Iver Terrace' in a similar morphological position, but with a different archaeological content. The morphological mapping of F K Hare (1947) showed that the type-sites of both the Furze Platt and Iver terraces lay beneath the same series of flats, which he chose to name the Lynch Hill terrace. In addition the lower gravel train was particularly flat in this area and consequently Hare felt justified in renaming it the Harefield terrace.

Besides the recognition of these extra units in the terrace succession, F K Hare (1947) also observed that the Harefield terrace, the Winter Hill terrace and the Taplow terrace each possessed a lower leaf or 'sub-facet'. Hare distinguished the sub-facets of the two higher terraces by the notations H_1 and WH_1 and named the lower leaf of the Boyn Hill terrace the

'Stoke Park Cut', but he did not give any designation to the lower division of the Taplow terrace because he doubted whether it deserved to be regarded as a separate feature. Subsequent mapping by K R Sealy and Catherine E Sealy (1956) carried the work of F K Hare westwards as far as the Goring Gap, and M F Thomas (1961) later extended the record into the Kennet and Blackwater-Loddon valleys. These workers showed that the sub-facets mapped by F K Hare in the Beaconsfield block, apart from the Stoke Park Cut, were widely developed in the middle Thames and its tributaries and so merited recognition as independent terraces. The H_1 sub-facet of the Harefield terrace was re-named the Rassler terrace by K R Sealy and Catherine E Sealy (1956), and the same authors used the terms 'Upper' and 'Lower' to describe the separate leaves of the Winter Hill and Taplow terraces. An analysis by E W H Culling of the long-profiles of the Chiltern streams (1956) confirmed the separate status of the upper and lower Taplow stages, and enabled him to identify an extra stage between the Boyn Hill terrace (his Boyn Hill I) and the Lynch Hill terrace. Culling believed the Stoke Park Cut might belong to this additional stage, which he called Boyn Hill II.

The preceding discussion of earlier research on the middle Thames terraces west of the Colne permits the terrace succession originally identified by F K Hare (1947) in the Beaconsfield block to be re-interpreted in the light of the later work of K R Sealy and Catherine E Sealy (1956) and E W H Culling (1956) in the following terms:

Stage II	Higher gravel train
	Harefield terrace
	Rassler terrace
	Upper Winter Hill terrace
	Lower Winter Hill terrace
	Black Park terrace
Stage III	Boyn Hill I terrace
	Boyn Hill II terrace (Stoke Park Cut)
	Lynch Hill terrace
	Upper Taplow terrace
	Lower Taplow terrace
	Flood plain

Terraces of the middle Thames east of the river Colne

The terrace record identified in the Beaconsfield block was traced eastwards as far as the mouth of the Brent during morphological mapping by the writer in 1973, thus completing the mapping of the terraces of the middle Thames begun by F K Hare (1947) and later extended westwards to the Goring Gap by K R Sealy and Catherine E Sealy (1956). An area comprising the north-eastern quarter of 10km grid square TQ07, the south-eastern quarter of grid square TQ08, the northern half of grid square TQ17 and the southern half of grid square TQ18 was mapped at a scale of 1:25000 using the technique adopted by K R Sealy and Catherine E Sealy in their continuation of the work of F K Hare upstream from the Beaconsfield Block. This method involves mapping only terrace flats (ie their nearly level surfaces) and 'slightly degraded terrace forms' (Sealy and Sealy, 1956, 370). A map showing the distribution of terrace flats in the eastern part of the middle Thames will be published in a later paper. This report includes a sketch-map (figure 5) indicating the disposition of the Thames terraces within the area outlined above. The terrace sequence in the greater part of this area has been discussed briefly by K R Sealy (1964, with map at figure 37), but the conclusions presented below differ from his analysis in several respects, most notably in our recognition of an extra unit, equivalent to the Stoke Park Cut of Hare (1947) and the Boyn Hill II terrace of E W H Culling (1956), here named the Stoke Park terrace.

Stage II deposits   *Lower gravel train, lower Winter Hill terrace and Black Park terrace*

Only a fragmentary record has been preserved of the Stage II terraces east of the Colne. The gravels at the summit of the Horsenden Hill (277ft (84m) OD; TQ163844) were included by S W Wooldridge within the lower gravel train, later renamed the Harefield terrace (Hare, 1947). The three terrace flats at Hillingdon (190ft (58m) OD; TQ070836, TQ072829, and TQ080830), underlain by deposits mapped by the Geological Survey as glacial gravels, were shown by Hare (1947) to mark the eastward continuation of the Black Park terrace. Another terrace flat at Uxbridge (199ft (61m) OD; TQ060849), a mile to the north-west, was stated by Hare to belong to the Black Park terrace of the Colne. The gravels capping Hanger Hill (204ft (62m) OD; TQ188821) seven miles downstream from the Black Park terrace at Hillingdon, and lying at a greater height, may belong to an earlier stage in the terrace succession and are here tentatively assigned to the lower Winter Hill terrace.

Stage III deposits   *Boyn Hill terrace, Stoke Park terrace, Lynch Hill terrace, Taplow terrace and Flood plain terrace*

Boyn Hill terrace   In the eastern part of the middle Thames the Boyn Hill terrace is far less widely developed than west of the Colne. The easternmost feature mapped by Hare (1947) as part of the Boyn Hill terrace in the Beaconsfield block was the terrace flat at Bangors Park, north of Iver (167ft (51m) OD; TQ030822). East of the Colne only two small adjacent flats at Moorcroft (TQ078817) and Hillingdon Heath (TQ079820) lying between 150ft–160ft (46–49m) OD, and the gravels at the top of Castlebar Hill (169ft (52m) OD; TQ171816), six miles to the east, have been referred to the Boyn Hill terrace, although several degraded summits lying between these two points and bevelled spurs on the western and southern slopes of Hanger Hill may also provide some indication of the course of the Thames at this time.

Stoke Park terrace When mapping the Beaconsfield block, F K Hare (1947) identified 'a curious erosion feature', which he named the Stoke Park Cut, extending from Farnham Royal to Black Park in an intermediate position between the Boyn Hill terrace and the Lynch Hill terrace. This sub-facet was interpreted by Hare as a meander terrace dating from the period of downcutting which followed the completion of the Boyn Hill terrace. Neither K R Sealy and Catherine E Sealy (1956) nor M F Thomas (1961) found any trace of this feature upstream from Bourne End, but E W H Culling (1956) was able to recognize an extra stage between the Boyn Hill stage (his Boyn Hill I) and the Lynch Hill stage in his investigation of the long-profiles of the Chiltern streams. He considered the Stoke Park Cut might represent this additional stage (his Boyn Hill II) within the Thames valley. In a recent discussion of the chronology of the Thames terraces P Evans reports the formation of flats related to pauses in the process of downcutting during the reworking of the Boyn Hill gravels at some localities along the lower Thames, and he refers to 'similar flats at Hillingdon and near Slough, the latter being the Stoke Park Cut' (Evans, 1971, 296). Mapping of the area east of the Colne has confirmed this view. There is clear evidence of an intermediate terrace in Hillingdon at Chapel Lane (TQ 075 810), Gouldsgreen (TQ 084 810) and Wood End Green (TQ 093 817) with its surface between 135 ft–140 ft (41–43 m) OD, lying at a higher level than the main

spread of the Lynch Hill terrace, yet below the Boyn Hill terrace at Moorcroft and Hillingdon Heath. The possible confusion arising from the application of the term 'Boyn Hill' to two independent terraces might be avoided if this usage is reserved for the upper unit alone, and the lower unit is termed the Stoke Park terrace. The section in Sabey's pits, Yiewsley (TQ 080 805) investigated by Desmond Collins and R N L B Hubbard (chapters 2, 3) exposed the Gouldsgreen gravels and overlying Gouldsgreen loam in the bluff of the Stoke Park terrace and extended down on to the rear of the Lynch Hill terrace. East of Yeading Brook this terrace is represented only by a small degraded remnant at Mount Pleasant (119 ft (36 m) OD; TQ 133 811), north of the Uxbridge Road at Hayes.

Lynch Hill terrace The easternmost feature mapped by F K Hare (1947) as part of the Lynch Hill terrace was the terrace flat at Richings Park, Iver (118 ft (36 m) OD; TQ 037 799), but he stated it could be seen to continue downstream to Norwood. In fact the continuity of the Lynch Hill terrace is broken at Norwood only by the local development of the Taplow terrace along both sides of the Brent, and the terrace can be recognized again at Drayton Green (TQ 160 810) and then traced through Ealing as far as Acton. East of the Colne, at Yiewsley and West Drayton, the surface of the Lynch Hill terrace, at the present day deeply scarred by sand and gravel working, lies at 105 ft–120 ft (32–37 m) OD. Between the Crane and the Brent the leading edge of this terrace drops below the 100 ft (30 m) contour, and to the rear it extends northwards past the Uxbridge Road into the valley of Yeading Brook. Beyond the Brent the Lynch Hill terrace, here divided into a series of isolated flats by

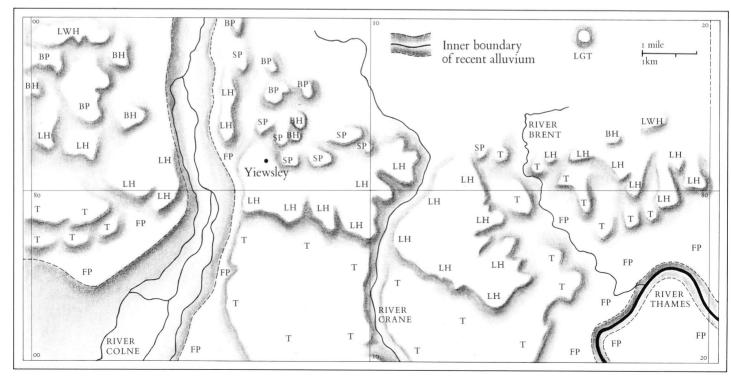

the shallow valleys of several small south-flowing streams, reaches 105 ft (32 m) OD at its inner edge near the British Rail (Western Region) main line, and descends to 89 ft (27 m) OD on the northern limit of Gunnersbury Park.

The Lynch Hill terrace in the eastern part of the middle Thames has long been renowned for the wealth of Lower and Middle Palaeolithic artefacts it has yielded to collectors. At an early stage in the archaeological investigation of this terrace J Allen Brown realized that implements of differing ages were stratified within different deposits (Brown, 1886; Brown, 1887; Brown, 1896; for detailed discussion of this and later work on the Lower Palaeolithic archaeology of the Yiewsley area see below). Also he was fortunate in finding implements associated with mammoth remains at both Norwood (TQ 139 793) and Southall (TQ 119 797) (Brown, 1888). The recent exposure at Sabey's pits revealed a sequence of four deposits at the rear of the Lynch Hill terrace, the basal Warrens gravel being followed by the Warrens loam then by the Stockley gravel and, finally, capping the succession, by the Stockley loam. These beds are described in greater detail in subsequent chapters.

Taplow terrace Recognition of the Lynch Hill terrace as a separate entity within the unit mapped by the Geological Survey as Taplow gravels has greatly reduced the area previously assigned to the Taplow terrace. Nevertheless, this terrace still remains the most widely developed feature in the terrace flight of the eastern part of the middle Thames. East of the Colne the main expanse of the Taplow terrace extends from Harmondsworth eastwards as far as Hounslow, the continuity being interrupted only by the valley of the Crane. On the southern boundary of London (Heathrow) Airport the surface of the Taplow terrace lies at 75 ft (23 m) OD, and the level gradually rises northwards until it reaches a height of 95 ft (29 m) OD just north of the M4 motorway. East of Hounslow the Taplow terrace narrows rapidly as the northward swing of the flood plain terrace around the large bend in the Thames at Kew approaches the Lynch Hill terrace at Osterley. Finally it becomes eliminated from the terrace succession at Gunnersbury, where the flood plain terrace impinges upon the Lynch Hill terrace. The Taplow terrace can, however, be traced northwards as a prominent shoulder along both sides of the valley of the Brent as far as Dormer's Wells and Hanwell. A small fragment of this terrace is also present south of the Thames at East Sheen (60 ft (18 m) OD; TQ 198 751).

In his discussion of the Chiltern stream profiles, E W H Culling (1956) predicted the upper Taplow (T_2) and lower Taplow (T_1) terraces would merge in the vicinity of Harmondsworth and he considered that the Taplow terrace downstream from that point would be represented in all probability only by the

lower Taplow (T_1) terrace. During mapping some evidence of the presence of an upper level within the Taplow terrace at Harmondsworth was encountered, but this has not been separated from the main body of this terrace on the sketch-map.

Flood plain terrace Investigation of the flood plain gravels during preparation of the one-inch new series geological map sheet 270 (South London: Drift) enabled H Dewey and C E N Bromehead (1922) to show that deposits of the low terrace had a composite origin, an earlier series of upper flood plain gravels being separated by the cutting of a buried channel from a later series of lower flood plain gravels, which had subsequently filled the channel to almost the same height. These two divisions could not always be distinguished in the field, but in at least one locality Dewey and Bromehead found a small bluff was present between them. In their discussion of the lower Thames Pleistocene sequence W B R King and K P Oakley (1936) described the formation of both an upper and lower flood plain terrace, and F E Zeuner (1945) believed the latter could be traced upstream beyond Brentford as far as Chertsey. Current mapping of the flood plain terrace between Brentford and Richmond has failed to reveal two distinct terraces separated by a bluff, although two different types of topography, which would seem to be equated with the upper and lower flood plain deposits of Dewey and Bromehead, are undoubtedly present.

Between Gunnersbury Park and Brentford End the bluff below the Taplow terrace gives place at a height of about 45 ft (14 m) OD to the more gently inclined surface of the brickearths of the upper flood plain deposits. At Brentford the brickearths have yielded an abundant mammalian fauna of last (Ipswichian) interglacial age, comprising hyaena, hippopotamus, red deer, giant deer, bos, bison and straight-tusked elephant (Zeuner, 1945). Within the large bend of the Thames at Kew and on the north bank of the river south of the London Road (A315) the upper flood plain brickearths are replaced by a complex system of low, whale-backed ridges, formerly eyots, rising to a height of about 25 ft (8 m) OD separated by shallow valleys. Similar topography has been reported from the flood plain further upstream (Hare, 1947) and also from the lower flood plain terrace along the lower Thames (King and Oakley, 1936). Mammalian remains indicative of cold climatic conditions have been obtained from this part of the terrace at several localities, most notably at Twickenham (Leeson and Laffan, 1894) and Isleworth (Callow, Baker and Pritchard, 1964; Callow, Baker and Hassall, 1966). At Willments pit, Isleworth (TQ 157 746) plant remains from a silt-bed beneath gravels yielding bison and reindeer have provided a finite radiocarbon date of 41 190 BC 43, 140 $\pm$ $^{1520}_{1280}$ BP (Birm–319) (Shotton and Williams,

FIGURE 5
Thames terraces in the vicinity of Yiewsley, mapped by T J Allen. The area west of the river Colne is based on the work of F K Hare and K R and C E Sealy

LGT Lower gravel train
LWH Lower Winter Hill
BP Black Park
BH Boyn Hill
SP Stoke Park
LH Lynch Hill
T Taplow
FP Flood plain

1973) suggesting the deposits of the flood plain terrace in this locality belong, at least in part, to the Upton Warren interstadial complex of the middle Devensian age. Apart from the alluvial flood plain of the Colne, referred by F K Hare (1947) to the flood plain terrace, recent alluvium is present within the eastern part of the middle Thames only to a very limited extent, being confined to narrow strips beside the Thames at Brentford and Kew, and along the valleys of the Brent and Crane.

Conclusion

The terrace succession mapped in the Beaconsfield block of F K Hare (1947) has been shown by recent mapping to extend downstream beyond the Colne into the eastern part of the middle Thames. Only three of the six Stage II terraces may be traced within this area, and then only as remnants of gravel capping isolated summits. All the Stage III terraces are present, including the extra unit identified by

F K Hare (1947) in the Beaconsfield block as the Stoke Park Cut which has been renamed the Stoke Park terrace in this chapter. The recent section in Sabey's pits, Yiewsley, exposed the Gouldsgreen gravel and Gouldsgreen loam in the bluff beneath this terrace and extended some way across the Lynch Hill terrace below, revealing the Warrens gravel, Warrens loam, Stockley gravel and Stockley loam. The pollen record and Palaeolithic archaeology of these deposits are discussed in later chapters.

Addendum Recent work on fossil insect remains from the biogenic silts at Isleworth has revealed that the climate was partly temperate for a short period near the beginning of the Upton Warren interstadial, though the environment was treeless and the 'cold' mammalian fauna present. COOPE, G R and ANGUS, R B. 1975. An ecological study of a temperate interlude in the middle of the last glaciation, based on fossil coleoptera from Isleworth. *Journal of Animal Ecology*, Vol.44 No.2, 365–391.

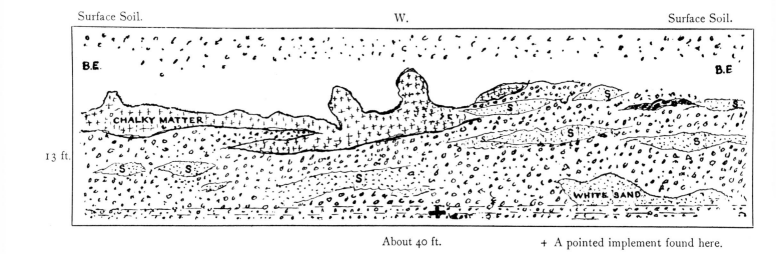

Surface Soil.   W.   Surface Soil.

B.E.   B.E

CHALKY MATTER

13 ft.

WHITE SAND

About 40 ft.   + A pointed implement found here.

Approximate scale in feet   Approximate scale in metres

Trail

Stockley loam (w4)

Coombe rock   ? Main Coombe rock

Stockley gravel (w3)

Warrens gravel (w1)

CHAPTER TWO

Terrace gravels, benches and stratigraphy of the Yiewsley area

Most of the Yiewsley area (figure 9) was covered by a spread of Pleistocene gravel at least 10 ft (3 m) thick; this in turn was usually overlain by brick-earths and solifluctions. The gravel, extensively worked between 1890 and 1960, ends to the west at the 100 ft (30 m) contour and the Colne valley. This contour is also the southern boundary. A large patch of the gravel is covered by government offices (at TQ 080 795), and from here eastwards and south of the railway little gravel has been dug and its extent is poorly known. North of the mainline railway, most of the gravel has been removed, but to the east of Dawley Road, in the area of the EMI factories for example, again little has been worked. Further east still, the terrace gravels seem to have been cut through by the Yeading Brook and the Brent, and they are hard to trace across Middlesex.

To the north of the Lynch Hill terrace is the Stoke Park terrace (see page 8), the bluff dividing them being close to the 125 ft (38 m) contour. This gravel spread is also bounded on the west by the Colne and on the east by the Yeading. To the north are other less extensive gravel spreads of the Black Park and perhaps also Boyn Hill terraces up to about 190 ft (58 m) at Hillingdon. These higher gravels form in effect an island surrounded by erosion.

The Lynch Hill gravel spread has an area of some 3 km² (1.2 mile²) west of Dawley Road; while the Stoke Park gravels cover about 2.6 km² (1 mile²). The putative Boyn Hill and Black Park gravels have an area of only some 0.5 km² (0.2 mile²) each.

By the canal about 20–25 ft (6–8 m) of deposits overlie the surface of the London clay, which is the bench of the Lynch Hill terrace. The ground surface is at 110 to 115 ft (33.5–35 m) and the bench is evidently close to 90 ft (27 m). In Warren Lake the Warrens gravel, reported to be some 20 ft (6 m) thick, had a surface at about 112 ft (34 m) OD, see figure 7b; therefore the bench here at the north-ern margin of the terrace was about 92 ft (28 m) OD.

The Stoke Park terrace has a higher bench, close to 120 ft (37 m) OD, and thus nearly 30 ft (9 m) higher than the Lynch Hill bench. The bench seems to have been fairly level at Yiewsley, for it is the bottom of Sabey's north-east pit by Barnes Farm, and the London clay had been scooped into at many points, though its surface was generally under water.

We can make a good estimate of the height of the surface of the Lynch Hill gravels (ie Warrens gravel,

w1). Near the canal it is near 100 ft (30 m) and the gravel is only 8 to 12 ft (2.5–3.5 m) thick. Clearly the reason why few pits are outside the 100 ft (30 m) contour is that once the 10 ft (3 m) or so of brickearth and solifluction is removed, there is not enough exploitable gravel left. In Warren Lake, the Warrens gravel has a surface at about 112 ft (34 m), but it rises to about 119 ft (36 m) where it abuts against the bluff.

The Gouldsgreen gravel has a surface at about 126 ft (38 m) OD at its southern margin and rises to a flat at about 131 ft (40 m) OD. It is not normally known how far below the modern surface the gravel surface lies, but here we have a long section where we know that the overlying deposit is between 2 and 4 ft (about 1 m) thick. This value may thus be regarded as a useful rule-of-thumb guide for estimat-ing the height of the gravel surface where only the land surface height is known and where no addi-tional Pleistocene deposit is thought to intervene.

J Allen Brown (1895a and b) and other workers have described the stratigraphy of the Lynch Hill terrace as consisting of 'stratified' (presumably fluviatile) gravel, overlain by 'unstratified' (pre-sumably solifluction) gravel, overlain by loams or brickearth; this is precisely the stratigraphy given for Maynard's pit.

Brown published sections of Eastwood's pit, and Pipkin's pit. The latter is reproduced in figure 6 together with an interpretation. The main strata were described by him as follows:

a. 'dense brown clay or brick-earth with trail' . . . apparently 4–6 ft (about 1.5 m) thick;
b. 'a very irregular deposit of chalk, rubble race and clay with a few stones in it, extending in tongue-like and wave-like forms into the clay' (figure 6a). This wave-like chalky deposit is clearly a solifluction and appears to be Coombe rock (a chalk solifluction deposit well known in the Thames valley). It seems from Brown's section that this chalky deposit was partly in and partly on top of a gravel layer which elsewhere he describes as 'the unstratified gravel'. The thickness of these two together appears to be 5–8 ft (1.5–2.5 m).
c. 'regularly stratified bed' of gravel, not well ex-posed in this pit. Its top was 11.5 ft (3.5 m) from the surface and there is evidence that it went down to 20–25 ft (6–7.5 m) below the surface; its thick-ness was thus sometimes in excess of 10 ft (3 m).

A fine section, over 1000 ft (323 m) long was recently exposed by H Sabey & Co in pits opened up since World War II (figure 7a).

This was drawn in 1972, and is reproduced here (figure 7b). Part of the section in the vicinity of the bluff is also shown in larger scale (figure 7c) because it is particularly complex. A further section was recorded (figure 7d) on the west face opposite this 34 m main east face section just mentioned.

FIGURE 7a

Map showing the position of the sections drawn in 1972 across the Stoke Park and Lynch Hill terraces

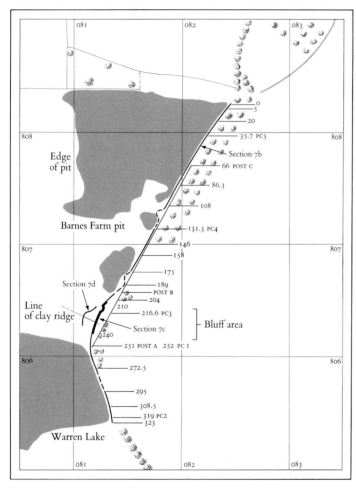

Notes to plan

Figures represent the distance along the section from its northern end, all in metres.

Grid lines at 100 metre intervals.

PC 1 to 5 = Pollen columns.

Posts A, B, C = Fence posts used in survey

FIGURE 7b

The 323-metre-long section exposed in the east faces of Warren Lake pit and Barnes Farm pit

Key to Sections

T	Top deposits
M	Modern deposits
B1	Orange sand
B2	Silver sand
B3	Grey clayey gravel
B4	Brown clay
G1	Orange gravel (Gouldsgreen gravel)
G2	White gravel
G3	Gouldsgreen loam
W1	Warrens gravel
W2	Warrens loam
W3	Coarse gravel (Stockley gravel)
W4	Stockley loam
LC	London clay
R	Ridge of London clay

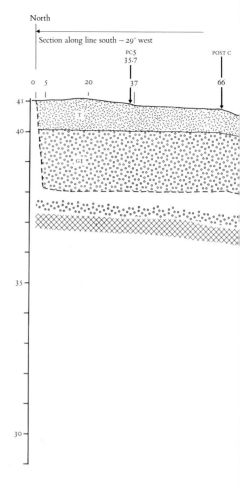

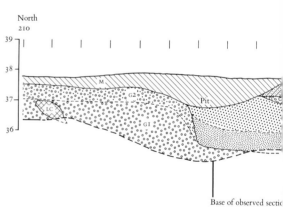

FIGURE 7c

Portion of long section between 210 and 244 metres in area of bluff and ridge, drawn and measured in detail

Notes to sections

Horizontal distances in metres from the northernmost point.

Heights in metres above OD.

PC 1 to 5 = Pollen column.

POSTS A, B, C = Fence posts used in survey

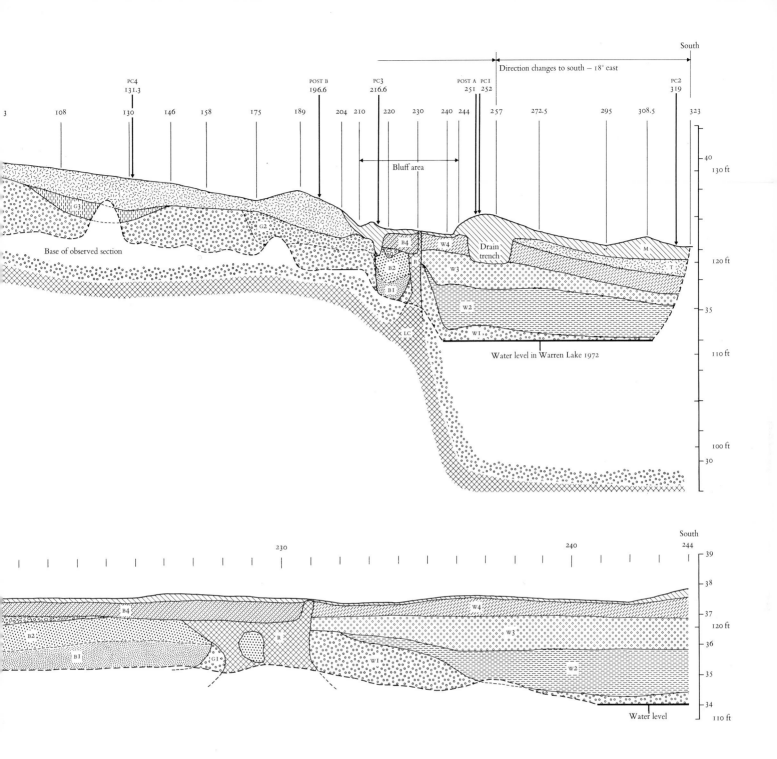

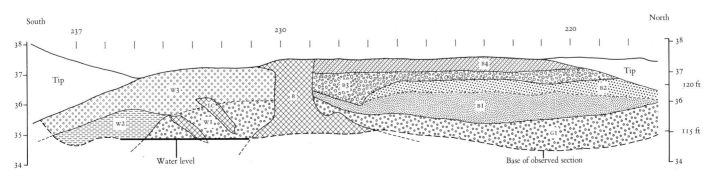

Figure 7d
Section opposite figure 7c in west face of cutting through bluff area

On the Stoke Park terrace, the Gouldsgreen gravel (G1) is exposed up to 7 ft (2.1 m) thick, but another 3–5 ft (1–1.5 m) must be added to carry the section down to the bottom of the partly flooded pit and to the London clay. A whitish gravel (G2), 3 ft (1 m) thick and probably a leached version of G1, is present near the bluff; elsewhere a pocket of sandy loam, the Gouldsgreen loam (G3), overlies G1. There are many bands of sand in the Gouldsgreen gravel: one in particular has characteristic black flecks, believed to be manganese. A number of reddened stones seem to have been burnt, but the nature of the fires believed to have caused this are unknown.

Immediately adjacent to the ridge of clay at the bluff between the terraces is a sequence of four deposits later than the Gouldsgreen gravel. They are B1, orange sand, 3 ft (1 m) thick; B2, silver sand, 2–3 ft (0.5–1 m) thick; B3, grey clayey gravel, 1 ft (0.3 m) thick, and lastly B4, brown clay, 2 ft (0.6 m) thick. This last is easily confused with the London clay, from which it is presumably derived and also with the Stockley loam (W4) to be described below.

The main deposit of the Lynch Hill terrace, the Warrens gravel (W1), is unfortunately mainly below the level of Warren Lake, which was 112 ft (34 m) OD when the section was drawn, but has since dropped a little. According to Sabeys the gravel was about 20 ft (6 m) thick. Against the clay ridge the Warrens gravel rises to 119 ft (36 m) OD. Above the Warrens gravel is the Warrens loam (W2), a sandy silt layer up to 5 ft (1.5 m) thick. In places it is divided into two roughly equal parts by a band of pebbles. Above this is the Stockley gravel (W3), an unstratified clayey gravel with stones at all angles. This is up to 4 ft (1.2 m) thick. Over this lies another more fine-grained loam, the Stockley loam (W4), up to 3 ft (1 m) thick. This is apparently weathered to clay, with prismatic cracks. Over this is a humic silt of probably post-glacial date (T), and rubble and dumped material (M).

There is probably a disconformity between W2 and W3, and a disconformity and weathering between W3 and W4. W1 is believed to be fluviatile, while W3 is believed to be a solifluction deposit. It is not clear whether W2 is fluviatile, implying a high river and sea level at this time, or colluvial (as W4 presumably is) implying a lower river level.

A section is also visible in Boyer's fishing lake (TQ 076 794). It has not yet been studied in detail, but there is at least 2 ft (0.6 m) of loam overlying a gravel, which is just visible above water level.

Position of the pollen samples

The stratigraphic position of the seven samples analysed for pollen is as follows: the two lowest samples, from the Gouldsgreen gravel (G1), were in

pollen column 5 (see figure 7b). Y-102 was taken at 40 cm from the top of G1, and Y-106 was 6 cm from the top of G1; the Gouldsgreen gravel was at least 1.5 m here. Y-92 was taken 6 cm from the top of the Gouldsgreen loam (G3) in pollen column 4; G3 was 38 cm thick here. Y-73, Y-68 and Y-66 were taken from pollen column 1; Y-73 was from the junction of the Warrens gravel (W1) and Warrens loam (W2), Y-68 was 1 m above the base of W2 (just below the gravel seam), and Y-66 was 1.3 m above the base of W2 and 25 cm below the base of W3. The only sample from the Stockley loam (W4) so far processed was taken between pollen columns 1 and 2, and was from about 20 cm above the base of W4 where it lies on W3.

Modern gravel digging at Sabey's pits, Yiewsley. Hand digging has been entirely replaced by mechanical methods

CHAPTER THREE

Pollen analysis of the Pleistocene deposits at Yiewsley: some interim results

By R N L B Hubbard

Summary

Analysis of samples from 4 of the series of deposits at Yiewsley shows that the pollen they contain appears to reflect open, meadow-like conditions accompanied by mixed oak forest (chapter 2). Unfortunately, it is not possible to say which of the various temperate periods that have occurred during the last few hundred thousand years are involved.

Preliminary palynological results for samples from most of the major geological members (figure 7b) of the Yiewsley sequence are presented in figure 8. In this diagram, samples separated by obvious stratigraphical discontinuities have been linked by broken lines. To achieve any results, a special preparation technique has to be used, because the recovered pollen concentration was less than 1000 grains per gram of dry soil. Physical methods allow removal of 90 per cent or more of the matrix before chemical methods of destruction are employed. Particularly clean preparations result, which are necessary if pollen is still to be visible after concentration from thirty or more grams of soil on to 1–4 microscope slides. Frenzel's technique of dense-liquid flotation (Frenzel, 1964) was employed because it is convenient, reliable, and well tested (Guillet and Planchais, 1969; Bastin and Coûteaux, 1966). This involves shaking the sample (after some preliminary chemical treatment) in a KI/CdI_2 solution of density 2.0 in which pollen grains float and minerals sink; the pollen is collected by filtration, and classical procedures of chemical preparation are then applied.

Two features are immediately obvious. Firstly, that despite the disparate contexts of the samples, results are essentially similar throughout the sequence. Secondly, the analysis seems to show an ecological association somewhat novel to the British Pleistocene – a mixture of temperate elements, trees and shrubs such as oak, elm, hazel etc, together with what would normally be considered a cool assemblage containing relatively high proportions of pine and birch, and consistently high non-arboreal pollen (NAP) counts.

In view of the very low concentrations encountered, and the fact that most of the deposits in question appear to have been water-lain, the first point to be considered is the significance of the results of this pollen analysis. Differential destruction of pollen can

apparently be discounted. There is no evidence of under-representation of the pollen types most susceptible to destruction; thus grasses (Godwin, 1958) and alder and hazel (Havinga, 1971) are all present. The 'mixed' nature of the floral assemblages means that secondary deposition of pollen must be considered – in this case since the 'cold' assemblage is always numerically dominant, the 'warm' component would have to be considered older and derived. The possibility of their appearance being connected with the redeposition of older sediments cannot be absolutely disproved, but it seems unlikely for a number of reasons. It would be a curious, but not impossible, coincidence if similar temperate deposits were being redeposited during each of the four different aggradational phases represented in the diagram. In the context of derived pollen, it is interesting to compare Yiewsley with the only English Rissian (*sensu lato*) pollen-diagram yet published – the Brandon Channel, Warwickshire (Kelly, 1968). In the Brandon Channel analysis, the temperate pollen, regarded as exotic, comprised 2–3 per cent of all pollen (Yiewsley: 10–20 per cent). Trees and shrubs amounted to 30–50 per cent (Yiewsley: 20–40 per cent), and pre-Quaternary spores were abundant, outnumbering the primary pollen (100–200 per cent of all pollen). At Yiewsley, on the other hand, no pre-Pleistocene pollen grains were definitely encountered. Further, to explain the arboreal pollen (AP) in Y–66, which consists largely of equal quantities of birch and oak pollen, by invoking the reworking of older sediments, calls for two pollen-rains as peculiar as the end product. Finally, the recovered pollen concentrations suggest either a very rapid rate of aggradation, or a very high rate of pollen destruction, (or both): the latter is almost certainly the dominating feature. This in itself makes the presence of large quantities of secondary pollen rather unlikely. Downwash from the present soil surface can be discounted since samples Y–108 and Y–77 from layer T contain a flora typical of soil pollen analyses of post-glacial soil profiles.

It appears then, that there are good reasons for accepting the evidence of figure 8 more or less as it stands. Some caution is necessary with regard to treatment of the calculated percentages, in view of the low and statistically inadequate counts, and it should be understood that we have little knowledge of the catchment and deposition (or re-deposition) of pollen by running water. Rowley and Walch (1972) however, have experimentally contaminated a stream with exotic pollen and studied the deposition; they concluded that the dispersal of such pollen is extremely complex, but not selective.

Very open conditions are indicated by the high NAP/AP ratio of 300 per cent. The presence of substantial proportions of oak, elm or hazel pollen, as well as of other thermophilous trees indicates temperate conditions. However, the relatively low proportions of hazel and willow suggests that the trees were distributed more as isolated extensive patches, rather than in the form of natural parkland. It could be argued that the openness of the conditions merely reflects a break in the tree-cover along the banks of a river.

The non-arboreal pollen (NAP) is almost invariably dominated by grass. *Rumex* types are the next most common herbs, (and in Y–66 they in fact dominate); the other types include Compositae, *Hypericum*, Umbelliferae, Leguminosae, Caryophyllaceae, *Urtica*, *Plantago sp*, Scrophulariaceae, Ericaceae, etc. This suggests the sort of tall weedy growth that could appear on almost any dry, open, disused, calcareous soil in England today. Arctic plants are absent. *Thalictrum*, which has a very distinctive pollen grain, and occurs regularly in glacial or interstadial pollen analysis – for instance from Brandon, Warwickshire; Chelford (Simpson and West, 1957); and Wookey Hole, Somerset (Tratman, Donovan, and Campbell, 1971) – is entirely absent. The sum of the *Artemisia* and Chenopodiaceae is plotted in figure 8 as a crude index of possible steppic character. Only in Y–63A and Y–66 did it approach 10 per cent of all pollen, and usually Chenopodiaceae outnumber *Artemisia*: this in striking contrast to Brandon, where *Artemisia* formed 3–13 per cent of the pollen sum.

Stoke Park terrace series

The conditions accompanying the deposition of the Gouldsgreen gravel (G1) seem to have been cool but temperate, with pine, birch, and oak the most common trees. Hornbeam is the only 'late interglacial' tree represented. After an uncertain time, and perhaps after some erosion of the Gouldsgreen gravel, the Gouldsgreen loam (G3) was deposited. This coarse, clayey sand could be regarded as chronologically intermediate between the aggradation of the Stoke Park terrace and the cutting of the Lynch Hill bench, or perhaps as part of the Stockley loam series (w4). It is linked to the latter by the high pine and low birch contents; but differs from it in its high elm and lime counts, and the lower proportions of hazel. The proportions of elm would seem to link the Gouldsgreen loam with the Warrens loam (w2), from which it is separated, however, by a major aggradational phase.

Lynch Hill terrace series

The bench of the Lynch Hill terrace was cut by a major lowering of the river level, presumably associated with a glacial advance subsequent to the aggradation of the Gouldsgreen gravels. It is to the Warrens gravel (w1) covering this bench that the huge collection of Acheulian implements, which stimulated this study, are believed to belong. Since the Warrens gravel is almost entirely below the present water-table, it has not yet been possible to take samples from the body of the gravel, and so to suggest the latest possible date for the implements. However, the overlying Warrens loam, consisting of clayey sand with a thin central band of small angular flint fragments, contains another undiagnostic, cool, temperate flora which is not helpful in correlation. Birch, oak, and elm are the most important tree types present, with pine playing a minor part and birch an increasingly important one. Hornbeam is again the only 'late interglacial' tree present. The thin band of angular flints has the appearance of being a solifluction deposit, as does the texturally similar Stockley gravel (w3) which caps the Warrens loam (w2): neither, however, is associated with ice-wedges or cryoturbation. Between them was found the remarkable association of birch and oak already commented upon. This sample was also anomalous in that it had unusually large quantities of dock and sorrel pollen, and unusually low grass percentages.

The Stockley loam (w4) is apparently a composite deposit. After the deposition of the Stockley gravel, the basal part of the Stockley loam seems to have been laid down under open conditions heavily dominated by grasses, and with pine and hazel the commonest woody species encountered – although the tree cover in fact would have been largely deciduous oak woodland. This deposit seems to have weathered to some degree resulting in a slight reddening, but was subsequently eroded so that less than half a metre now remains. Overlying it is a silt deposit which is presumed to be a post-glacial slope-wash, since a sample from a depth of about 70 cm (Y–77) contained 90 per cent NAP with grasses heavily outnumbered by other herbs, elm, alder, birch, pine, hazel, and a large quantity of fern spores – a class of plants otherwise almost entirely absent. There were also many charcoal fragments, reflecting man's activities.

There would appear to be two alternative interpretations for the pollen diagram (figure 8):

a. an open, riverine facies of the established interglacial floras or

b. a series of novel temperate periods within 'glacial' episodes.

Sadly, the layers and their pollen content as shown in figure 8 cannot easily or reliably be correlated with known climatic events. This is partly the result of their incomplete nature; but even after more work on the Gouldsgreen gravels, the Warrens loam, and the Stockley gravel to establish the floral dynamics, the fragmented nature of the geological sequence may rule out much further clarification. No diagnostic pollen types were encountered, or only at uninformative frequencies; and while it is just possible that pollen types such as yew and juniper might have been overlooked given the conditions of preservation, types such as spruce and fir, which extend some way into the Wolstonian at Marks Tey (Turner, 1970), could not. Our knowledge of English glacial floral sequences is extremely limited, since most of the deposits are absent, or are not susceptible to treatment by traditional methods of pollen sample preparation; and the Quaternary sequences that have been studied often lack even the late interglacial stages. Finally, while in Britain only two temperate stages are at present recognized between 'Mindel' and 'Würm', on the continent four or five such stages have been observed. Zagwijn and others (1971) have hinted at a pre-Holsteinian interglacial, whilst Menke (1968) has described a post-Holsteinian interglacial at Wacken in Schleswig-Holstein, and Erd (1970) has described an inter-Saale interglacial sequence at Kap Arkona, Rügen, on the Baltic coast of Germany, as well as both Holstein and Dömnitz interglacials. Surprises, therefore, are perhaps to be expected.

One correlation, albeit tenuous, that can be attempted, is with the upper loam at Swanscombe (Hubbard, unpublished), where one sample (LAI–1.20) gave results that are in some ways reminiscent of sample Y–66:

	LAI–1.20	Y–66
Pinus	2 per cent	– per cent
Betula	53	42
Alnus	33	–
Quercus	5	37
Ulmus	5	11
Tilia	2	5
Carpinus	–	5
Corylus	28	11
Juniperus	2	–
Rhamnus	–	5
Total sample on which above percentages based	110	19
Non-arboreal pollen	70 per cent	67 per cent
Gramineae	46	25
Total sample on which above percentages based	432	67
Pollen concentration (grains per gram of soil)	38	2.0

These two samples clearly differ in many important respects. However, they have in common (other than their peculiarity):

a. the combination of unusually high birch and very low pine counts;

b. the mixture of about 50 per cent birch with about 50 per cent temperate deciduous forest elements;

c. quite low proportions of shrubs to trees;

d. high non-arboreal pollen (NAP) counts.

Birch, of course, is a tree that is particularly capable of anomalous behaviour in pollen-diagrams as a result of its propensities as a pioneer colonist of cleared ground. Unexpectedly high birch counts, and low proportions of temperate trees occur, however, in other related samples. Since the results of the analyses of these samples have at present no obvious parallels in the British Pleistocene record, it is perhaps reasonable to conclude (pending further evidence) that the samples Y–66 and LAI–1.20 belong to approximately the same period in time.

The Stockley gravel, then, would correspond to the upper gravel at Swanscombe, which unlike the former is associated with periglacial phenomena. The Warrens gravel might be equivalent to the Swanscombe upper middle gravel – which would make good archaeological sense. The Gouldsgreen gravel might then in turn either correspond to the lower middle gravels, or to the lower gravels at Swanscombe: the latter, however, differ by containing lower pine and birch proportions, much lower oak, and vastly higher elm counts (Hubbard, unpublished).

It is very hard to equate the pollen analysis from the lower part of the Stockley loam with the Ipswichian interglacial: if it had to be done, a late Zone II (Jessen zone e/f) date would appear to be the most probable correlation. It certainly bears no relationship to the early Devensian as represented at Chelford. A return to the conditions prevalent during the deposition of the Warrens loam seems more likely.

A final point concerns the pollen preservation. The samples were moderately to slightly acid (pH values in the range of 4.7–6.5). Above pH 6.0 it has been found that pollen preservation in surface mineral soils rapidly becomes too poor for pollen analysis (Dimbleby, 1957). Thus in the neutral or alkaline soils (pH values 7.0 and higher) the preservation is very bad. On the basis of the measured pH values and Dimbleby's findings, the pollen concentration might be expected to lie in the region of 2000–800 000 grains per gram of soil, in some cases at least – rather than the 1–4 grains per gram actually found at Yiewsley. It must be concluded that during deposition the geological formations at Yiewsley were distinctly alkaline (which would account for the rarity of Ericaceae pollen), and that the acidification is a relatively recent development.

Addendum Further research has shown that the Yiewsley pollen-spectra seem to be typical of deposits laid down by running water in any interglacial period. The terrace aggradations in the lower Thames valley seem to belong to interglacial zone II times.

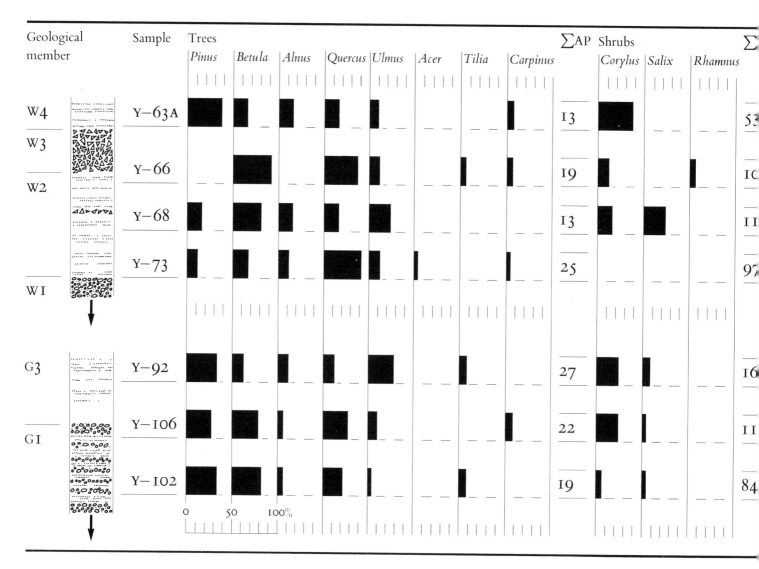

Geological member	Sample	Trees								∑AP	Shrubs			∑
		Pinus	Betula	Alnus	Quercus	Ulmus	Acer	Tilia	Carpinus		Corylus	Salix	Rhamnus	
W4	Y–63A									13				53
W3														
	Y–66									19				10
W2														
	Y–68									13				11
	Y–73									25				97
WI														
G3	Y–92									27				16
	Y–106									22				11
GI	Y–102									19				84

0   50   100%

A selection of some of the better preserved and more photogenic fossil pollen grains recovered from the sands and gravels at Yiewsley. All are reproduced at a magnification of ×780. The pointer in the three left-hand photographs indicates the position of structural features which are important in identification, but which were not readily visible in these photographs. The *Pinus* pollen grain is a composite of two photographs of the same grain taken at slightly different planes of focus

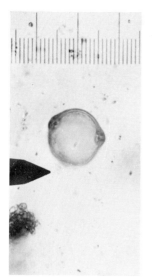

Betula

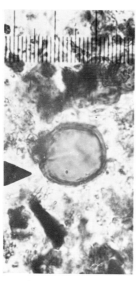

Corylus

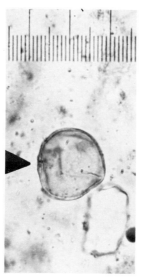

Gramineae

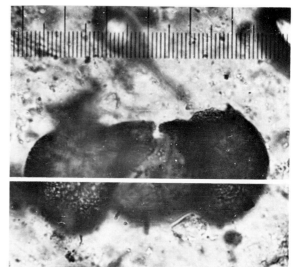

Pinus

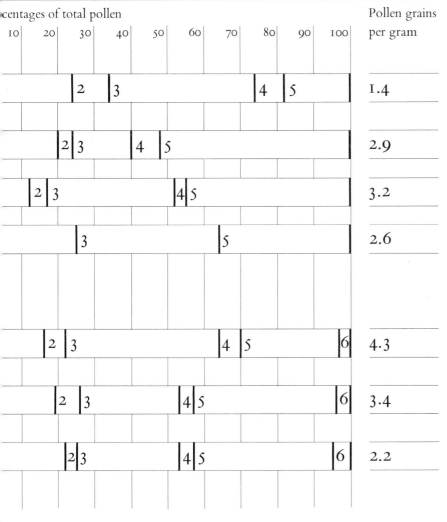

	Pollen grains per gram
	1.4
	2.9
	3.2
	2.6
	4.3
	3.4
	2.2

FIGURE 8
Diagram of pollen frequencies from successive Yiewsley deposits and photographs of pollen grains.

G1 and G3 are the Gouldsgreen gravel and loam of the higher (Stoke Park) terrace. W1 and W2 are the Warrens gravel and Warrens loam of the lower (Lynch Hill) terrace. W3 is the Stockley gravel (solifluction) and W4 the Stockley loam.

The thickness of the column for each tree can be read as a percentage of the total tree pollen from the scale given at the bottom

ΣAP is the sum of all the tree pollen

Σ is the sum of all pollen

1 Trees
2 Shrubs
3 Gramineae
4 Chenopodiaceae plus *Artemisia*
5 Herbs
6 Ericaceae

Botanical families and species named here

BOTANICAL NAME	COMMON NAME
Abies	Fir
Alnus	Alder
Artemisia	Mugwort
Betula	Birch
Carpinus	Hornbeam
Caryophyllaceae	Pinks and campions
Chenopodiaceae	Goosefoot family
Compositae	Daisies and dandelions
Corylus	Hazel
Ericaceae	Heaths and heathers
Gramineae	Grasses
Hypericum	St John's wort
Juniperus	Juniper
Leguminosae	Vetches
Picea	Spruce
Pinus	Pine
Plantago spp	Plantains
Quercus	Oak
Rhamnus	Buckthorn
Rumex	Docks and sorrels
Salix	Willow
Scrophulariaceae	Figwort family
Taxus	Yew
Thalictrum	Meadow rue
Tilia	Lime
Ulmus	Elm
Umbelliferae	Hedge parsley
Urtica	Nettle

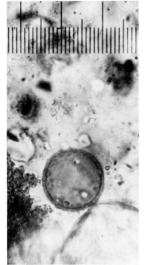

Plantago

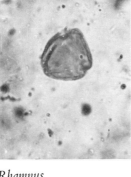

Rhamnus

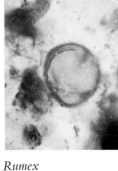

Rumex

CHAPTER FOUR

Pleistocene chronology of the Yiewsley area, and its correlation with other areas

Mammal and molluscan fossils are absent from the Yiewsley deposits, probably because decalcification has resulted in too high a level of acidity. Upstream of London, the terraces above the Taplow terrace rarely have fauna associated with palaeoliths. There is a report of horse and giant deer (*Megaceros*) from the handaxe-bearing Lynch Hill gravels at Cannoncourt Farm, Furze Platt, near Maidenhead and Baker's Farm, near Slough. Some fauna is known from Datchet Reservoir (TQ 000 770) only 5 km from Yiewsley; this includes elephant and deer, but it is from no higher than the upper flood plain terrace. We do know that the Lynch Hill terrace is earlier than the upper flood plain terrace which is last interglacial on faunal and palaeobotanical grounds, but because there is so little fauna in terraces higher than the flood plain terrace it is of limited use in dating.

Pollen seems likely to provide a more useful guide to correlation. The nearest Pleistocene sequences are Trafalgar Square (Franks, 1960) and Ilford (West and others, 1964) for the Ipswichian interglacial, and Hatfield (Sparks and others, 1969) and Marks Tey (Turner, 1970) for the preceding Hoxnian interglacial. Pollen work is going ahead at Swanscombe and Stoke Newington and, together with further analysis from the Yiewsley area, this should make correlation much easier.

The geological sequence at Yiewsley, which seems to follow the main boulder clay episode in the Thames basin (the Finchley and Aldenham lobes) is as shown in table 2.

A longer sequence for this part of the middle Thames is provided by the terrace scheme elaborated by Wooldridge, Hare and others, and discussed by Allen (page 7). Assuming that each terrace represents a true geological cycle, this gives at least 12 stages. The terraces are listed in column 1 of table 3 for a cross-section of the Thames valley along the line separating grid squares SU and TQ.

Correlation of Pleistocene sequences

I would like to make it clear that the correlations implied in table 3 (also Collins, 1969, 1971 and 1976) do not represent the views of T J Allen or R N L B Hubbard, my colleagues; they will in due course elaborate their own views, and are not to be held responsible for any correlations here.

TABLE 2 The Pleistocene sequence at Yiewsley

	Post-Lynch Hill	
Stockley stage	{	Deposition of Stockley loam (?colluvial) and trail in Eastwood's pit (?solifluidal) Deposition of Stockley gravel (solifluidal) and ?Coombe rock
	Lynch Hill cycle	
Warrens stage	{	Deposition of Warrens loam (?colluvial) Deposition of Warrens gravel (fluviatile) Cutting of bench at 90 ft (27 m) OD
	Stoke Park cycle	
Gouldsgreen stage	{	Deposition of Gouldsgreen loam Deposition of Gouldsgreen gravel (fluviatile) Cutting of bench (by erosion) at 120 ft (37 m) OD

Correlation may be attempted with local, regional or general sequences. The most appropriate local sequence is that for the Swanscombe area (Ovey [ed.], 1964; Collins, 1969, 1971 and 1976) in column 3. The appropriate regional sequence for the lower Thames is that of King and Oakley (1936) reproduced with modification in column 4. Column 5 records conventional correlation with the standard British sequence (Mitchell, Penny, Shotton and West, 1973) which is based mainly on East Anglia (West, 1968). Column 6 has the standard sequence proposed for north-west Europe (Subcommission for European Quaternary Stratigraphy; Luttig, 1968). Archaeologists continue to use the 'Alpine' terminology. This is not based on correlations with deposits or units of the original type area, the Alpenvorland of South Germany, but rather on a series of agreed (or disagreed) equivalents (see column 7).

I believe that correlation is necessary in order to facilitate many kinds of worthwhile Palaeolithic research, and cannot be overlooked simply because it is controversial. At the same time it must be stressed that among the varied views which exist on regional and time correlation, a number seem quite irreconcilable. Table 3 depends partly on a rather well-known model of Pleistocene correlation especially associated with the work of Oakley and West; in my opinion this is close to the truth. This network of conclusions cannot be argued in detail here but three of its principal elements are as follows:

a. the high terrace river deposits of Barnfield pit, Swanscombe represent only one main interglacial (as opposed to several);

b. this Swanscombe interglacial is correlated with the Hoxnian (of Hoxne, Clacton, Nechells etc);

c. the Hoxnian interglacial of Britain is equivalent in time to the Holstein (*sensu stricto*) interglacial of north-west Europe.

There are many alternative correlations of the Pleistocene which, although I do not personally favour them, cannot easily be refuted. If new research should show that any of these variants (eg that the

Hoxnian is not equivalent to the Holstein) are preferable, modification in the correlations here would be required; the table is so constructed that it is easy to do this.

Correlation of the Yiewsley stages and the construction of a time-scale can be attempted using the following lines of evidence to suggest equivalents or to test competing versions: the terrace sequence; the more characteristic stratigraphic units; the pollen evidence (analyses for which are still only at a preliminary stage); and the archaeological sequence. Its position in the middle Thames terrace sequence has already been discussed, and is not in real doubt. Correlation with the lower Thames, especially the

TABLE 3   Yiewsley's place in local, regional and general sequences

Thames terraces and related events [1]	Yiewsley stages [2]	Swanscombe stages [3]	Lower Thames stages [4]	British standard sequence [5]	Warm or cold	North-west European standard sequence	Alpine name
Alluvium	Hillwash	Springhead peat	XVII Tilbury	Flandrian	w	Flandrian	
Lower floodplain	Trail	Uppermost loam (loess)	XV Slades Green	Devensian	c	Weichselian	Wurm
	Stockley loam						
Upper flood plain		Temperate bed	XII Crayford	Ipswichian	w	Eemian	
Taplow		Ebbsfleet middle and lower loams (loesses)	XI 'Taplow-Endsleigh'	Wolstonian	c	Saalian	Riss
Main Coombe rock	Stockley gravel	Main Coombe rock	X Baker's Hole				
Lynch Hill	Warrens loam Warrens gravel	Barnfield upper loam and middle gravel	VIII Middle Barnfield	Hoxnian	w	Holsteinian	
Stoke Park	Gouldsgreen loam Gouldsgreen gravel	Barnfield lower loam and lower gravel	V Lower Barnfield				
Boyn Hill							
Black Park							
Main glaciation			III Great eastern glaciation	Anglian	c	Elsterian	Mindel
Winter Hill							
Rassler							
Harefield							
Higher gravel train			I 'Plateau'	Cromerian	w	'Cromer'	
Pebble gravel				Beestonian	c		
				Pastonian	w		
				Baventian	c	Menapian	
				Antian	w	Waalian	Gunz
				Thurnian	c	Eburonian	
Netley Heath				Ludhamian	w	Tiglian	
				Waltonian	c	Pretiglian	

1 Mainly Wooldridge and Hare.
2 See table 2.
3 Ovey, ed, 1964; and others.
4 Simplified from King and Oakley (1936), omitting erosional and other stages.
5 Mitchell and others, 1973.

Swanscombe area, and perhaps later the Stoke Newington area, seems most fruitful. Using Swanscombe as an intermediary, correlation with the East Anglian sequence (the standard British sequence) can be attempted.

At present it is not easy to correlate the river terrace at Swanscombe (lower and middle gravels) with the terraces of the middle Thames. It is almost certainly not the Boyn Hill terrace (*sensu stricto*). It may be the Lynch Hill terrace or the Stoke Park terrace or both (Collins, 1976). The view that both terraces may be present is taken here. Further work on the terrace surfaces, benches and gravels is planned to clarify this.

The pollen sequence through the Gouldsgreen stage (G1 and G3) is to be expanded, but I provisionally conclude that it might be equated with the sequence through the Swanscombe lower gravel and loam (Hubbard, unpublished). Similarities are the hazel rise, and alder overtaking oak in frequency; pine-birch-alder-oak-elm are continuous in both, and arboreal pollen (AP) is surprisingly low (under 50 per cent and often 15–30 per cent). On the other hand there are dissimilarities; Gouldsgreen has higher birch and pine, and less elm. There is no trace of yew which was continuously present in the upper part of the Swanscombe lower loam. Possibly the equivalent level at Yiewsley was higher in the Gouldsgreen loam and has been eroded away. The rise of hazel to moderate values and the increase of alder relative to oak at Swanscombe and at Yiewsley would fit Hoxnian zones IIa and b (West, 1968), as would the continuous presence of yew at Swanscombe. Yew is characteristic of Hoxnian zone IIc. Differences from the Hoxnian are the high elm and high non-arboreal pollen (NAP) ratings, though NAP was intermittently high at Hatfield, the locality nearest to Yiewsley that is attributed to the Hoxnian interglacial.

The association of a high percentage of non-arboreal pollen with a continuous presence of oak and other associated thermophilous trees poses a problem. This will need further investigation; possibly the type of sediment or the unconventional techniques of preparation have something to do with this anomaly; or we may have a new non-Hoxnian phase with its own special climate; or human interference may be relevant. Reddened stones were common in the Gouldsgreen stage probably indicating fires. It is known (Collins, 1969) that Lower Palaeolithic man often preferred open environments: he may even have been responsible for destroying some of the forest cover by burning or felling the trees.

As stated by Hubbard (page 17), there appear to be interesting similarities between Swanscombe upper loam and Warrens loam. Sample Y–66, for instance, with the unusual combination of very high birch frequencies, thermophilous trees and negligible pine, resembles Swanscombe upper loam (LA1) with the same characteristics. The Stockley loam pollen sample, probably Late Pleistocene, is not at present easily matched. At this stage it should be admitted that my preferences on correlation have been heavily influenced by the archaeological sequence discussed in chapter 10, where it is argued that the Clactonian, Barnfield, Cuxton and Northfleet stone tool assemblage-types are found in the same order as at Swanscombe. The deposits associated with these assemblage-types seem to correspond well also.

The Stockley gravel and Coombe rock, with a Northfleet-type (tortoise core and Levallois flake) assemblage, matches the Baker's Hole main Coombe rock assemblage (and probably equivalent Craylands Lane and Barnfield upper gravels), all at Swanscombe. The top of the Warrens gravel, and probably the Warrens loam, having a Cuxton(I+II)-type assemblage, matches the top of the Swanscombe middle gravels and upper loam; in both cases the gravels are followed by a loam which may be colluvial. Beneath this, fluviatile gravels at both sites (Swanscombe middle gravels and Warrens gravel) have a Barnfield-type of Acheulian assemblage.

At Swanscombe, and probably at Yiewsley, the Acheulian is preceded by Clactonian (Swanscombe lower gravels and Gouldsgreen gravel), and the two are separated by a lowered river level and downcutting. Lastly it may be noted that the Swanscombe terrace in the lower Thames is preceded by a main glacial episode (Hornchurch boulder clay), while in the middle Thames the Yiewsley sequence is preceded by what is almost certainly the same Thames valley glaciation (the Finchley and Aldenham boulder clays, which are contemporary with, or earlier than, the Black Park terrace). These coincidences seem sufficiently remarkable to justify a correlation.

Whereas at the moment the British sequence has no well-studied temperate periods between the Hoxnian and the Ipswichian, in north Germany Erd and Čepek (1969) have two: the Dömnitzian (a second Holstein [*sensu lato*] interglacial) and the Rügenian (an inter-saale [*sensu lato*] interglacial). The Pritzwalk vegetation sequence covers the cool period (Fühnian) between the Holsteinian and Dömnitzian. This includes the following vegetational associations: birch-juniper; pine–willow; and a high NAP tundra vegetation. As a long range correlation, the birch-juniper of Swanscombe upper loam LA1, and the pine–willow of Warrens loam (Y–68) might be Fühnian or early Dömnitzian in date. A pollen spectrum from the Steinheim gravels (Holstein [*sensu lato*]) also has the pine–willow association. More work, especially including the discovery of a Dömnitzian interglacial in Britain, would make it easier to evaluate these suggestions. The rarity of such a Dömnitzian would easily be explained by the falling sea level of that period which would have caused erosion to predominate.

CHAPTER FIVE

Location of pits from which Palaeolithic stone tools have come

The first collector known to have worked in the Yiewsley area was Mr John Allen Brown. He obtained palaeoliths from Maynard's and Odell's pits as early as 1889, and continued collecting until about 1901, mainly in these pits and Eastwood's pit. The artefacts were mostly labelled Dawley or Hillingdon. Brown's collection was purchased by Dr Sturge and passed to the British Museum (Smith, 1931).

In 1905, the next major collector, Mr R G Rice, began acquiring material from Eastwood's, Boyer's, Maynard's and Wallington's pits. From 1908 to 1916 he collected from Clayton's pit, and from 1914 to 1917 from the Western Cartage Company's pit. The other pits remained prolific at least until 1929. Rice was already 52 when he began collecting in 1905 and by 1929 he was 76. On his death at the age of 80 his collection went to the London Museum. Obviously old age was one factor which brought his collecting to a halt. Vulliamy (1930) also points out that mechanical diggers came into use between 1928 and 1930, and the hand digging which had been the source of so many palaeoliths came to an end.

Other collectors were Major Fred Sadler, the Acton Borough Surveyor, whose finds went to Gunnersbury House Museum in 1923; and F N Haward who also collected between the wars. A note was published by J G Marsden (1928) on the stratigraphy of his finds. A D Lacaille (1938) noted a tool from de Salis' pit, but unfortunately the pit is not located, nor are any other pits described or located. Lacaille continued collecting after World War II in Sabey's pits, and especially in the Chapel Lane area to the north-east. It is unfortunate that throughout this long period of investigation, the published references have been very thin. Our attempt to reconstruct the pits' locations appears in figure 9.

Brown (1895a, 119) stated that 'Odell's pit' was to be reached by proceeding along the canal from Hayes station. The labels on several artefacts described this pit as being south of the canal. It could hardly have been anywhere other than in the triangle between Dawley Road on the east, the canal on the north and the mainline railway on the south (figure 9). Since maps of the 1930s show Dawley House and its orchards covering part of this, two small remaining areas (TQ 087 799) and (TQ 085 798) are the likely positions. Possibly both were part of Odell's pit. Subsequently the area became railway sidings.

There is no direct record of the position of 'Clayton's pit'. 'Odell's' was one of Brown's richest sources of palaeoliths and yet it was not mentioned by Rice. On the other hand, 'Clayton's' was, up to 1916, one of Rice's richest pits although not mentioned by Brown. Since Rice usually collected from the same pits as Brown, it seems very likely that these two names refer to the same pit. The fact that a turning off Dawley Road, opposite Odell's site, is called Clayton Road would appear to support this. The railway sidings, built over the supposed site of 'Clayton's/Odell's pit' by the 1930s, would explain why finds ceased here about 1916, if that is the date of the sidings.

Judging by the account of Brown's field excursion with the Geologists' Association on 4 May 1895, 'Maynard's', 'Pipkin's' and 'Eastwood's' pits were in a line from east to west on the northern side of the canal and not far from it. Rice labelled 'Maynard's pit' as 'Yiewsley', while Brown described it as being at 'Dawley' and said that 'Maynard's' pits were extensive. It seems likely that they were between the gasholders (TQ 083 803) and the canal. The older pits were usually served by a 'dock' or canal branch, so that gravels could be transported by barge; the dock (now filled) at TQ 084 802 could have been the centre of Maynard's exploitation. There is also some evidence, discussed below, that part of Maynard's pits may have been as far west as TQ 080 803 or TQ 080 801.

'Pipkin's pit' was by the canal, and was probably close to the local district boundary (between Yiewsley and Dawley) running through TQ 080 800 roughly north-south. Possible locations are at TQ 081 799, just east of the line, or TQ 079 799, just west of the line, or both. This pit has the most complete recorded section of the early pits, but was not rich in artefacts.

'Eastwood's pit' was the richest in the area, with over 1300 artefacts in the Rice Collection alone. We know from Rice's labelling that this pit was taken over by H Sabey and Co between December 1925 and April 1926. Sabey's pits, I am informed by the company, have hitherto all been north of the canal, and west of the local boundary with Dawley and the gasholders. Almost certainly 'Eastwood's pit' was in the oblong area around TQ 077 800, some 350 × 200 m, and known to the gravel diggers as 'Sabey's Foresters pit', because it is opposite the *Foresters* public house. The only other possible location near the canal would be the strip west of Stockley Road, around

TQ 075 800, but this does not fit the descriptions so convincingly.

If Sabeys took over Pipkin's pit, it was probably close to TQ 080 800, and if they took over Maynard's, this is likely to have been near TQ 081 803. Rice labelled some artefacts 'Sabey's New pit at Stockley' in the years 1926 to 1928. These new pits were probably west of Stockley Road, most likely the ballast pits marked near TQ 074 804 on the fifth edition of the one-inch map, at the head of a dock now filled in. With the introduction of mechanical digging about 1930, Sabeys speeded up the gravel digging, and almost the entire spread of gravel west of Stockley Road has been exploited. The northern part near Chapel Lane was being finished about 1970, when our work was beginning. Rice's 'Yiewsley pit', which was not rich, may have been near the dock at TQ 072 801, the nearest point to Yiewsley village.

The second most prolific, and perhaps the most elusive, pit is 'Boyer's'. Just as 'Sabey's' is often misspelt 'Sabery's' by the old collectors, 'Boyer's' is often misspelt 'Bowyer's'. Messrs William Boyer and Sons is still a large firm operating pits. Apparently, since World War II, there has been a simple division between Sabey's pits occupying all the area north of the canal, (except George Cross's pit by the gasholders, which was finished by the 1960s) and Boyer's pits which were all south of the canal and railway. Boyers still own much land south of the canal. Their most recent pit, now a fishing lake (TQ 076 795), was dug in the 1960s. On the 1949 air photos, none of the area east of Stockley Road seems to have been touched, so the pits at TQ 077 972 were probably worked in the 1950s. It is possible that the triangle east of Stockley Road, south of the canal and railway and north-west of the dock (TQ 078 797) has been exploited, but probably only the brickearth was removed. The 1949 air photo does not indicate pits, and this area is now a factory estate.

The alternative siting for the old 'Boyer's pit' is west of Stockley Road and south of the railway, where Boyers still own much land. Taking only the spread of gravel above the 100 ft (30 m) contour, this area falls into a northern portion, now covered by a housing estate centred on Briar Way and built about 1949, and a more southerly area bounded by the canal dock on the north and the 100 ft (30 m) contour on the south and west. Mr Dew, of Hillingdon Borough Engineer's Department, informed us that the Briar Way estate was not built on backfilled gravel pits, but brickearth was being removed here before 1890. Clearly the palaeoliths recorded by Rice between 1905 and 1929 are not likely to be from the Briar Way end. In the 1949 air photo, much of the southern area is occupied by water-filled pits dug in the 1940s or earlier; but they are not on the fifth edition of the one-inch map, which does show brickworks beside the dock. Boyer's pit of 1905 to 1929 is

most likely to have been near the canal and Starveall Farm at about TQ 074 795. In 1910 a series of Late Bronze Age urns were found by Rice in the same pit in the topsoil at the edge of a gravel pit, but the locality was never described in detail (Vulliamy, 1930). 'Broad and Co's brickfield' (also 'Broad and Harris') is probably the brickfield where Briar Way estate now stands. On one tool it is described as 'Starveall'; Starveall Farm is at TQ 076 795.

The area north of the Foresters pit is called '24-acre field'. Part had been dug in 1949, but the remaining gravel east of Stockley Road and north of grid line 803 has been worked since. In the 1950s the present Warren Lake was dug by mechanical grab. Six handaxes were recovered about 1955 (figure 10). In the 1960s almost the entire area up to Gouldsgreen, except for some causeways and a strip by the road, was dug. A few artefacts have been found. At the time of writing (1973) the gravel of Barnes Farm (TQ 083 818) is being dug away.

At present the best sections, and the most interesting opportunities for study, are in the east end of Warren Lake and in the pit to the north near Barnes Farm, now being extended. A series of test bores were made in the field at TQ 083 806, to the east on the Dawley side of the boundary, and this may soon be dug.

FIGURE 9
Location of the pits mentioned in the text. The position of some of the pits is conjectural

View of the east end of Warren Lake. The southern end of the 1972 long section is visible above water level

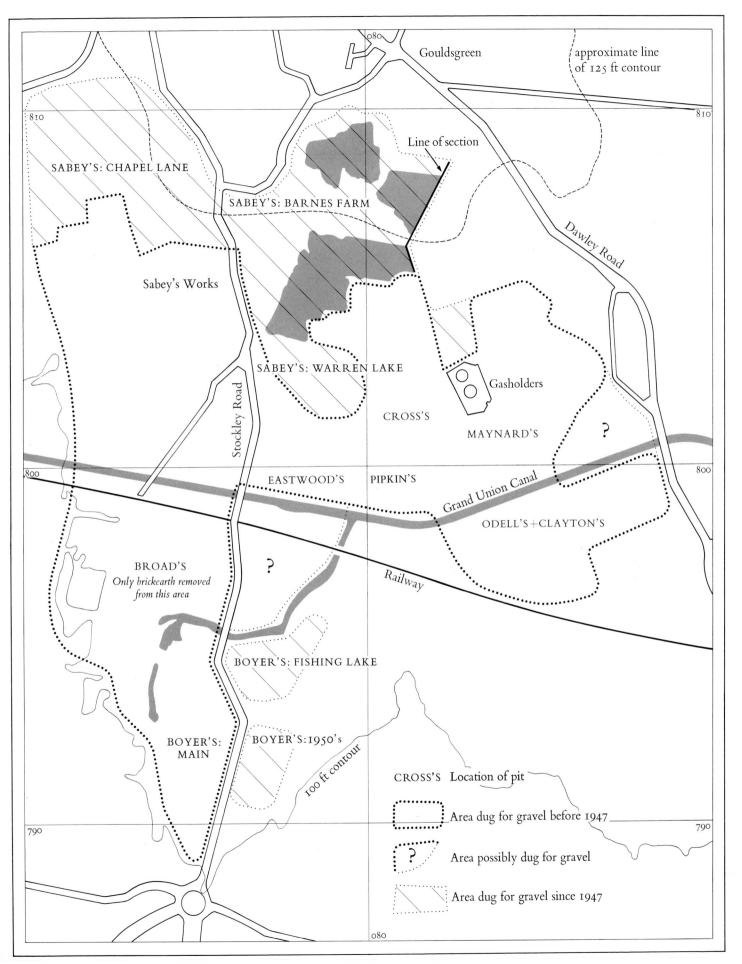

Gouldsgreen

approximate line
of 125 ft contour

810

SABEY'S: CHAPEL LANE

Line of section

SABEY'S: BARNES FARM

Dawley Road

Sabey's Works

Sabey's: Warren Lake

SABEY'S: WARREN LAKE

Stockley Road

Gasholders

CROSS'S

MAYNARD'S

?

800

EASTWOOD'S   PIPKIN'S

Grand Union Canal

ODELL'S + CLAYTON'S

BROAD'S
*Only brickearth removed
from this area*

?

Railway

BOYER'S: FISHING LAKE

BOYER'S:
MAIN

BOYER'S: 1950's

100 ft contour

CROSS'S   Location of pit

Area dug for gravel before 1947

?   Area possibly dug for gravel

Area dug for gravel since 1947

790

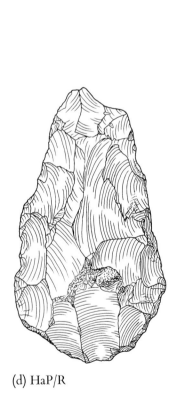

(a) HaS

(b) HaC

(c) HaC

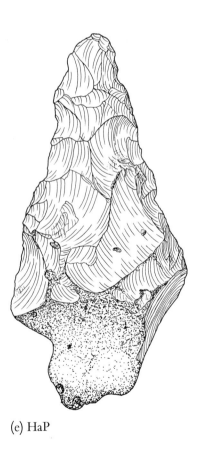

(d) HaP/R

(e) HaP

(f) HaP

FIGURE 10
Six handaxes from
Warren Lake, found
about 1955

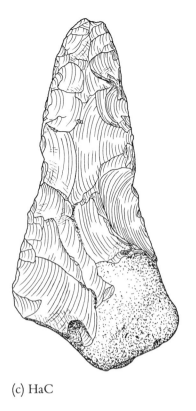
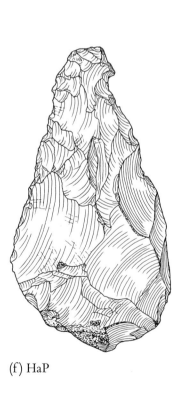
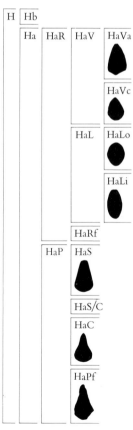

H	Hb			
	Ha	HaR	HaV	HaVa
				HaVc
			HaL	HaLo
				HaLi
			HaRf	
		HaP	HaS	
			HaS/C	
			HaC	
			HaPf	

Handaxe types
See figure 13, page 32,
for fuller explanation

All stone tools are
reproduced at half size,
unless otherwise stated

CHAPTER SIX

The Rice Collection

Robert Garraway Rice died on 10 January 1933 at the age of 80. He had been a Fellow of the Society of Antiquaries since 1891 and was Vice-President in 1924-6. He collected over 2600 palaeoliths in the Yiewsley area from 1905 to 1929 or thereabouts, and he marked them with the name of the pit, the date of acquisition and his name. He seems to have visited the pits regularly throughout the period, but more during the summer months than the winter. It is presumed that he bought the specimens from the workmen, but he collected flakes as well as handaxes, and there is such a high proportion of rough flakes and poor handaxes that any selection for 'belles pièces' seems unlikely. More likely a few of the best specimens they had found were sold by the workmen elsewhere or to other collectors.

Apart from a few pieces which went to the British Museum, it seems that the entire collection of palaeoliths went to the London Museum (now the Museum of London) in 1933. A small number of pieces, unmarked by Rice at his death and presumably found between 1929 and 1932, were marked by the London Museum in 1934. At present 64 of the artefacts from the museum, including 27 handaxes, are deposited on loan at the Institute of Archaeology in Gordon Square, London.

A count (table 4) gives the total as 2601 artefacts: 1336 from 'Eastwood's pit', 948 from 'Boyer's pit', 94 from 'Clayton's pit', 45 from 'Maynard's pit', 77 from 'Western Cartage Co's pit', 30 from 'Sabey's "new" pit' and 71 from 'Yiewsley pit', 'Wallington's pit' and other unspecified Yiewsley localities. In 1905 Rice labelled all the pits as 'West Drayton', but from 1906 onwards artefacts from all these pits, some 99 per cent of his collection, were marked Yiewsley.

Almost all the palaeoliths are made of flint. The source of this flint has not been investigated, but it was probably very local and certainly mainly derived from the upper chalk. Flint would have been carried eastwards from the chalk by several terrace stages preceding the Lynch Hill. The condition of the tools varies from distinctly rolled to almost fresh, but a slightly worn or smoothed condition is commonest for the handaxes, while a near fresh condition is more typical of the Levallois flakes; but the range of both overlaps considerably. Most handaxes and flakes are iron-stained. Patination colours include brown, orange or, most often, brownish-yellow, and quite often a curious grey-yellow colour.

There is one undoubtedly different and much rarer patination group, of white to bluish-white colour, sometimes with 'basket work' patina on them. The typology and stratigraphic position of this series is discussed below. There are only about 11 examples of this group in the Rice collection. Another patination group can be distinguished with less confidence. It is buff or lightish in colour and rather fresh. As explained below it consists mainly of Levallois blades and flakes with 'chapeau-de-gendarme' butts. It is difficult to give numbers for this group as it grades into the stained series on one side and the bluish-white series on the other, and the most economic view is to group it with the latter.

The main part of the Rice Collection will be analysed as a single unit below. This is not because it is believed to come from a single level, but because the two or three levels likely to be present cannot be adequately distinguished in the collection. The view that some three stages of the Acheulian are present is elaborated below.

TABLE 4   Analysis of the Rice Collection

Types of artefact and notation [1]		Yiewsley pits: Eastwood's	Boyer's	Clayton's	Maynard's	Western Cartage Company	Sabey's New pit	Other pits	Total
Main divisions									
Levallois flakes	DL[1]	178	176	11	2	7	7	7	388
Other flakes	E+F	413	334	46	14	55	17	23	902
Cores	C	31	9	1		1	1	4	47
Handaxes [2]	H[1]	703	413	32	28	14	5	34	1229
Tools [3]	B[1]	7	12	4				1	24
Bluish-white series		4	4		1			2	11
Total		1336	948	94	45	77	30	71	2601
Analysis of cores									
Levallois cores	CL[1]	18	6	1		1	1	1	28
Total cores	C	31	9	1		1	1	4	47
Analysis of handaxes									
Handaxes [2]	H[1]	703	413	32	28	14	5	34	1229
Typical handaxes	HaT	301	204	30	26	13	5	19	598
'Pointed'	HaP	102	68	11	14	5	1	10	211
Concave sides	HaC	24	16	2	4			3	49
Straight sides	HaS	19	9	7	7	1	1	1	45
'Rounded'	HaR	187	134	19	12	6	4	8	370
Long cordiform	HaVa	85	50	7	4	6	2	4	158
Short cordiform	HaVc	23	13	7	4			1	48
All cordiforms	HaV	167	113	18	10	6	3	7	324
Limande	HaLi	5	8		1		1		15
Ovate	HaLo	7	5	1	1				14
Oval group	HaL	16	18	1	2		1	1	39
S–twists		8	6	1				1	16
Cleaver tips		7	5						12
HaP index		35.3	33.6	36.6	52.0				
Analysis of tools									
Tools [3]	B[1]	7	12	4				1	24
Retouched (Acheulian) notch	Jb		2	1					3
'Knives' retouch-backed	Ka		1						1
'Knives' natural or cortex	Kc	1	2	1				1	5
Racloir	R	5	3	2					10
Grattoir	L	1	3						4
Levallois point	DP		1						1

1 Author's notation for types in accordance with Collins (1969, 1970a) and figure 13.

2 This figure includes roughouts and untypical handaxes.

3 Tools excluding handaxes (class H).

CHAPTER SEVEN

Typology of handaxes and other tool types in the Rice Collection

The handaxe is by far the most numerous tool type in Rice's Yiewsley collection. There were 1229 handaxes found as against only 24 other tools. The latter included 3 notches of the retouched (Acheulian) type (figure 11a), 5 natural or cortex-backed knives (figure 11b, c, d) and one rough retouch-backed knife (figure 11e). The remainder consisted of 4 grattoirs ('endscrapers') (figure 11f, g), 10 racloirs ('sidescrapers') (figure 11h, i, j) and one Levallois point. The latter seems to belong to the buff series and could therefore be separated out. The retouched notches and knives are, of course, typical in the Acheulian context. The racloir-grattoir group are not, in my opinion, of much diagnostic value; the racloirs were not of Quina type and Clactonian and Charentian types were conspicuously absent.

The problems of handaxe typology are far from solved. All workers agree that, within the general class of handaxes, there are characteristically different shapes or types. The most authoritative subdivision is that of Bordes (1961). However, there are no universally used English equivalents of his names (such as *ficron*) and the Bordes types are not ideal for the kind of analysis used here, there being, for example, no convenient designation for the handaxes with straight or concave sides, here called HaP.

Since 1969 I have used notations for handaxe types and groups (Collins, 1969; 1970). This system, outlined below, should not be regarded as finally fixed, but is intended for improvement by modification. The handaxe totals for each pit are given in table 4, with a subsidiary figure for typical handaxes, excluding roughouts, broken or untypical specimens. For the richer pits this reduces the figure by a half, and is a good indication that the collection is not biased towards better specimens. As explained below, the percentage of handaxes in the 'pointed' or ficron group (HaP; see figure 13) seems to be important. There are 102 of this group from Eastwood's, while typical non-pointed or rounded handaxes (HaR) from the same pit number 187. The HaP index (HaP/HaP+HaR×100%) is accordingly 35.2 (102/102+187×100%). The 187 HaR handaxes belong mainly to the cordiform (HaV) group with 167. The remainder of the 187 is made up of the limande-ovate group (HaL), with only 16 typical specimens, and 4 specimens indeterminate between HaV and HaL. S-twists (figure 15d) were rare in Eastwood's (which had 8) and cleaver tips rarer still with only 7.

The breakdown of the handaxes from Boyer's pit shows a great similarity with those from Eastwood's, as also does the smaller collection from Clayton's. The figures from Maynard's are a little different, with higher HaP index (52.0) and no S-twists. A possible explanation is given in the next section.

Cores are generally rare in all pits. This is typical of the Acheulian. Indeed cores are rare in most Lower Palaeolithic sites in Britain. However, the total of tortoise cores (figure 18) from the Yiewsley sites (28 in the Rice Collection) is the largest such assemblage after Baker's Hole and this is clearly different from other stages with handaxes. The richer pits all produced Levallois flakes (figure 20) and the number of faceted butts was high. The Levallois flakes were typically ovate (figure 20b, c, f) or subovate. The more laminar examples (figure 22d) with highly faceted 'châpeau-de-gendarme' butts are believed to belong to the buff-coloured series. One Levallois point (figure 22e) belonged to the buff series and 2 to the bluish-white series. A few of the regular Levallois ovates had extensive lateral retouch (figure 22h) as found at Baker's Hole.

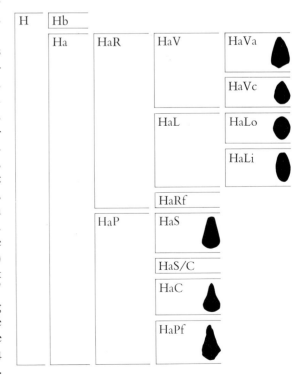

Handaxe types
See figure 13, page 32, for fuller explanation

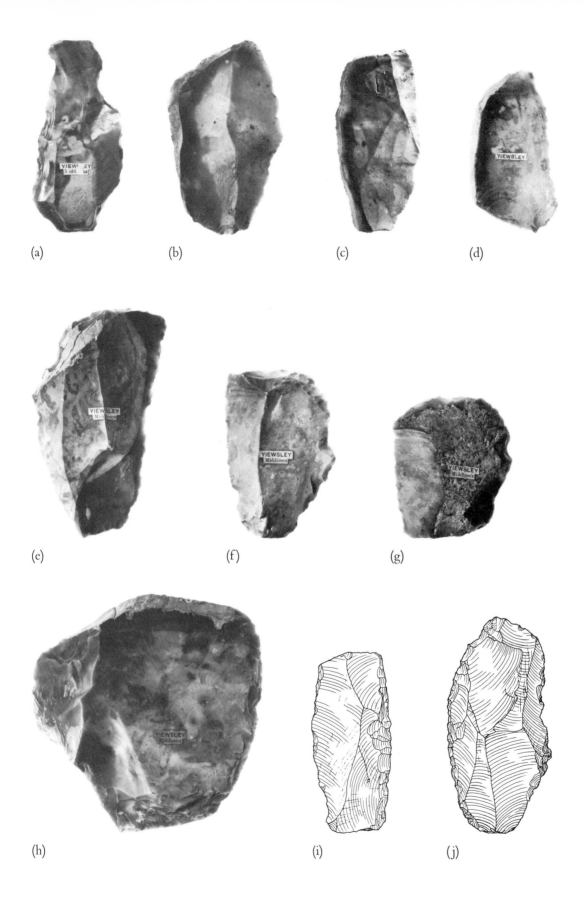

(a)

(b)

(c)

(d)

(e)

(f)

(g)

(h)

(i)

(j)

FIGURE 11
Tool types from
Yiewsley, Rice
Collection

(a) Retouched notch
(b,c,d) Cortex backed
knives
(e) Irregular backed
knife
(f,g) Grattoirs
('endscrapers')
(h) Racloir
('sidescraper')
(i) Racloir on
Levallois blade
(j) Racloir on Levallois
flake

All stone tools are
reproduced at half size,
unless otherwise stated

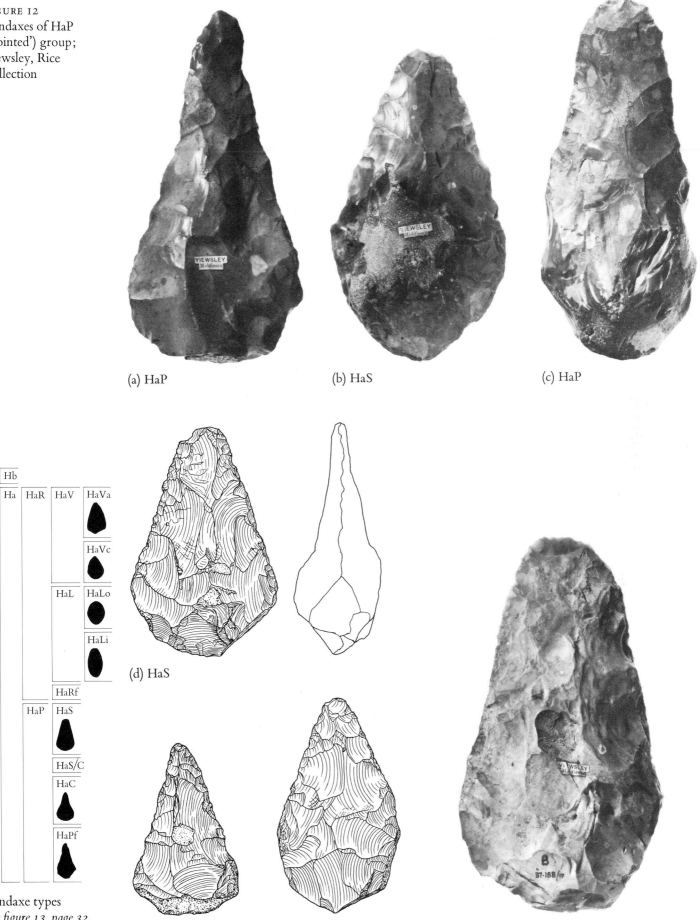

FIGURE 12
Handaxes of HaP
('pointed') group;
Yiewsley, Rice
Collection

(a) HaP

(b) HaS

(c) HaP

H	Hb			
	Ha	HaR	HaV	HaVa
				HaVc
			HaL	HaLo
				HaLi
		HaRf		
	HaP	HaS		
		HaS/C		
		HaC		
		HaPf		

(d) HaS

Handaxe types
*See figure 13, page 32,
for fuller explanation*

(e) HaS

(f) HaS

(g) HaS

H	Hb				
Handaxes	Roughouts, untypical forms and handaxe-like objects				

FIGURE 13
System of breakdown of handaxe types.
The categories to the left are made up by totalling those to their right

Ha	HaR	HaV	HaVa	
Typical handaxes	Total of HaL and HaV	*Cordiform (general)* Handaxes with convex sides having their widest point near the base	*Elongated and Amygdaloid Cordiform* Long forms of HaV	

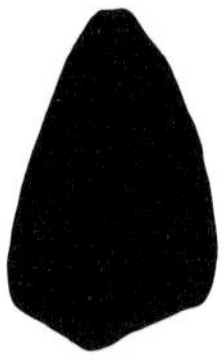

			HaVc	Paxton-type
			Standard Cordiform Short or ordinary forms of HaV including Paxton-type handaxes	

		HaL	HaLo	
		Handaxes with convex sides having their widest point near the middle	*Ovate* Short forms of HaL	

			HaLi	
			Limande Long forms of HaL	

HaRf
Handaxes not easily attributed to HaL or HaV but definitely convex sided

HaP	HaS	
Total of HaC and HaS	*Lanceolate* Handaxes with pointed shaft whose sides are straight	*Metrical definitions of long and short types exist but are not widely used*

HaS/C
Handaxes with a combination of straight and concave sides

HaC
Micoquian
Handaxes with pointed shaft whose sides (from widest point to tip) are concave

HaPf
Ficron
Handaxes not easily attributed to HaC or HaS but definitely pointed shaft

Bordes' equivalents appear in italics

FIGURE 14
Handaxes of HaR
('rounded') group;
Yiewsley, Rice
Collection

(a) HaV

(b) HaVa

(c) HaVa

(d) HaVa

(e) HaVa

(f) HaV

(g) HaVa

All stone tools are
reproduced at half size,
unless otherwise stated

FIGURE 15
Handaxes of HaR
group; Yiewsley, Rice
Collection

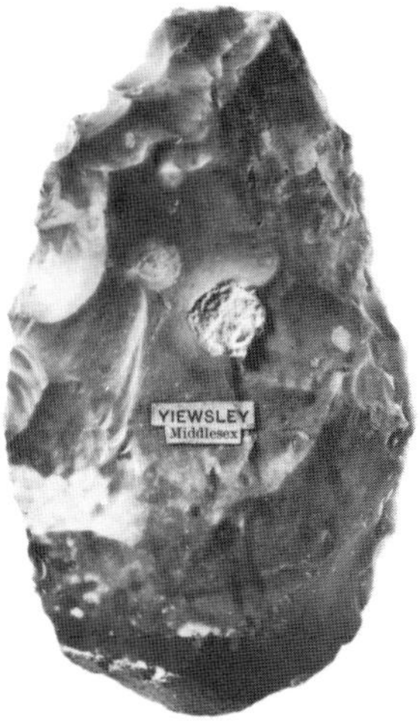

(a) HaV

(b) HaVc

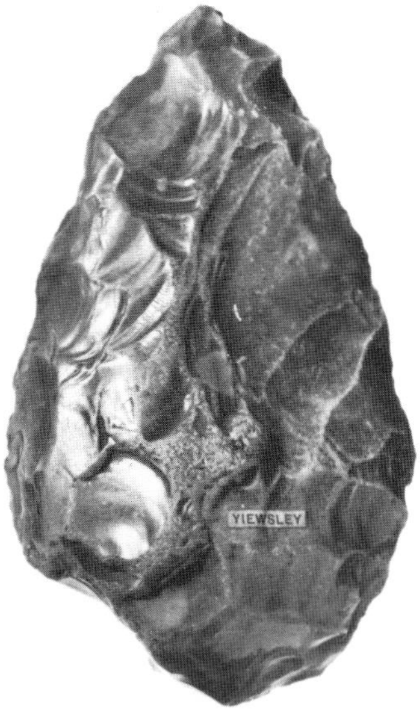

(c) HaV

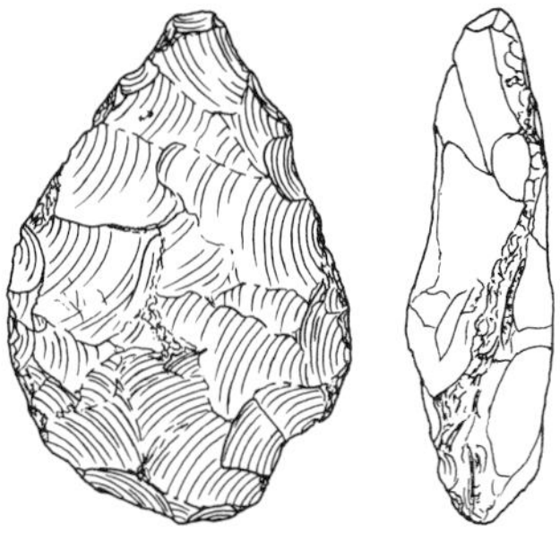

(d) HaVc   twisted

(e) HaVc

(f) HaVc

(g) HaVc

(h) HaV

(i) HaV

(j) HaVc

(k) HaVc

(l) HaVc rolled and
atypical

All stone tools are
reproduced at half size,
unless otherwise stated

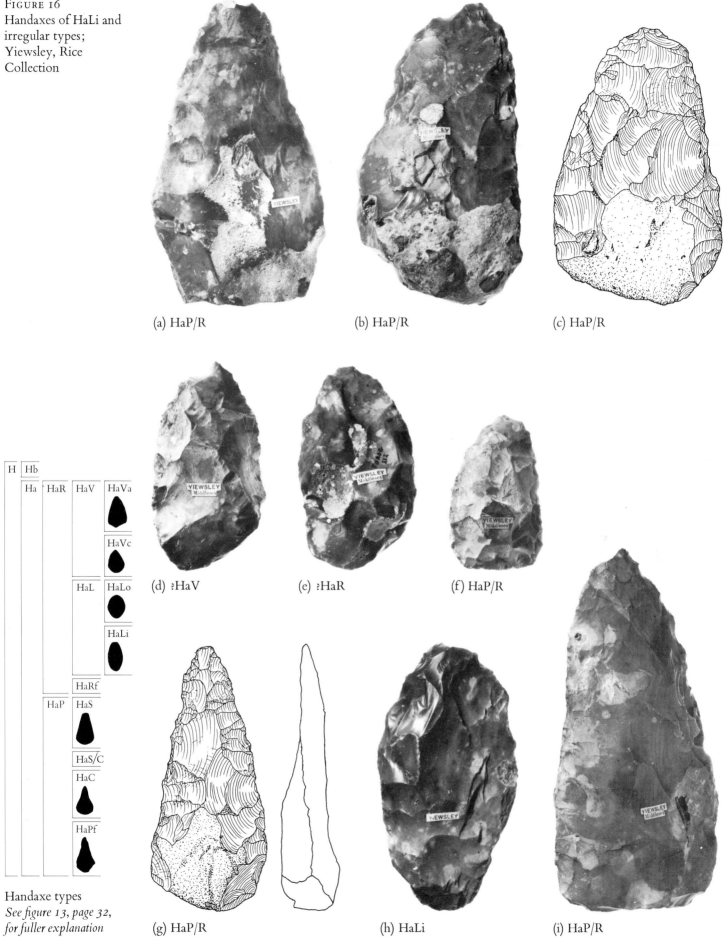

(a) HaP/R

(b) HaP/R

(c) HaP/R

(d) ?HaV

(e) ?HaR

(f) HaP/R

Handaxe types
*See figure 13, page 32,
for fuller explanation*

(g) HaP/R

(h) HaLi

(i) HaP/R

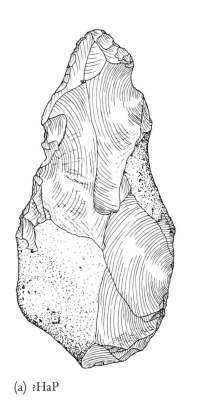

(a) ?HaP

(b) ?HaV

(c) ?HaV

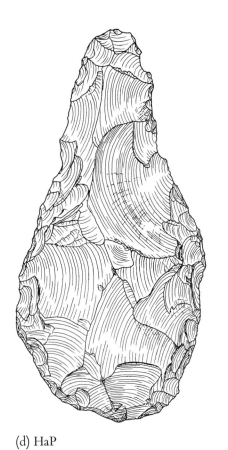

(d) HaP

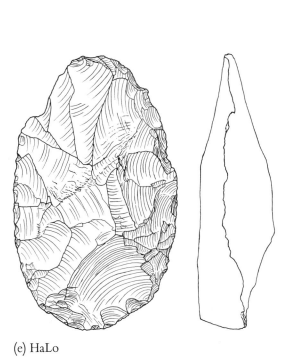

(e) HaLo

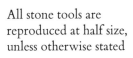

All stone tools are
reproduced at half size,
unless otherwise stated

Handaxe types
*See figure 13, page 32,
for fuller explanation*

H	Hb			
	Ha	HaR	HaV	HaVa
				HaVc
			HaL	HaLo
				HaLi
			HaRf	
		HaP	HaS	
			HaS/C	
			HaC	
			HaPf	

FIGURE 18
Tortoise cores;
Yiewsley, Rice
Collection

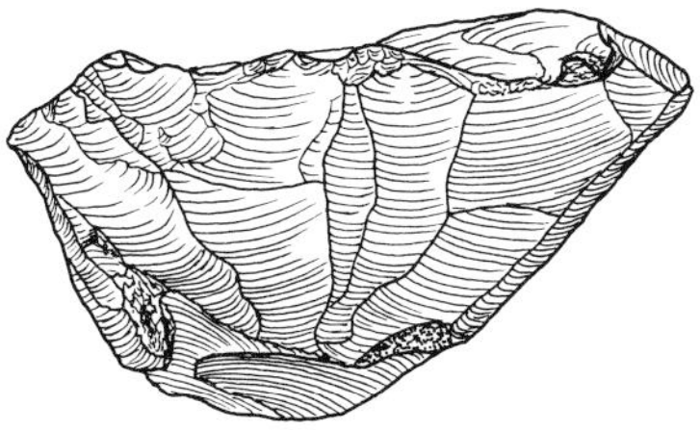

(a) four views

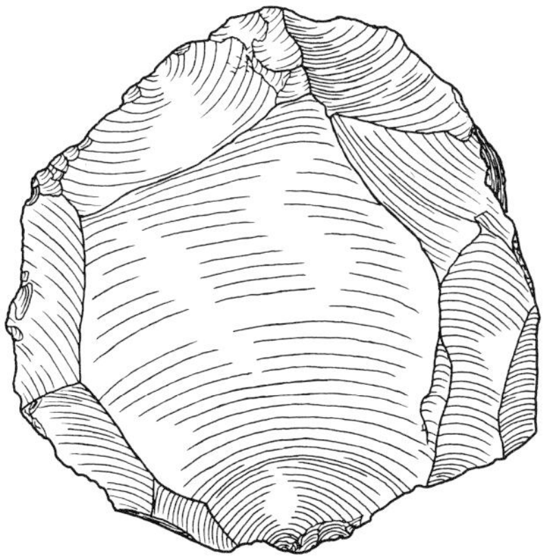

(b)

(c) two views

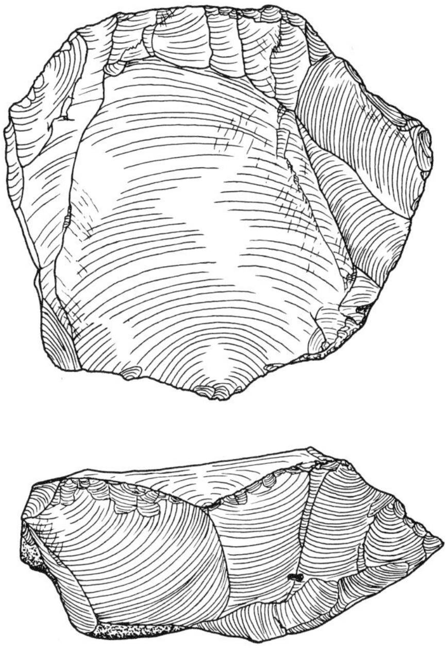

(d) two views

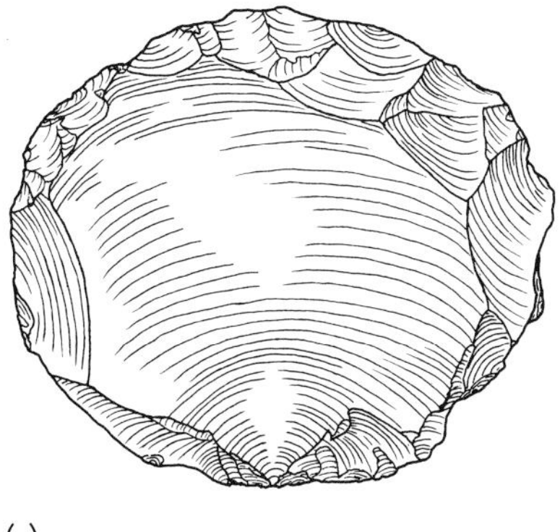

(e)

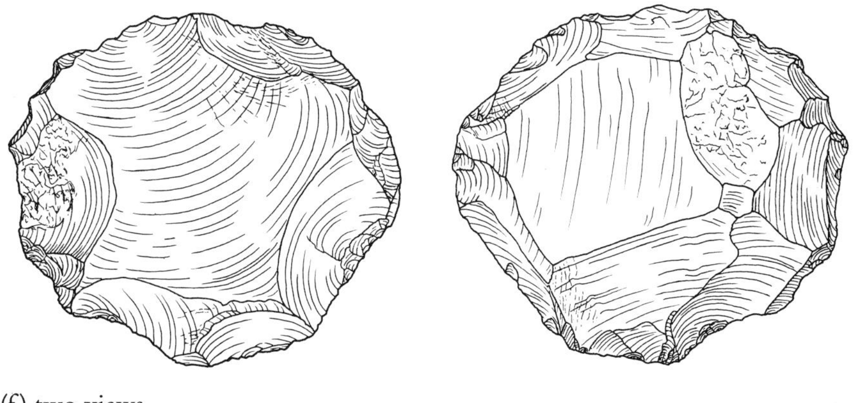

(f) two views

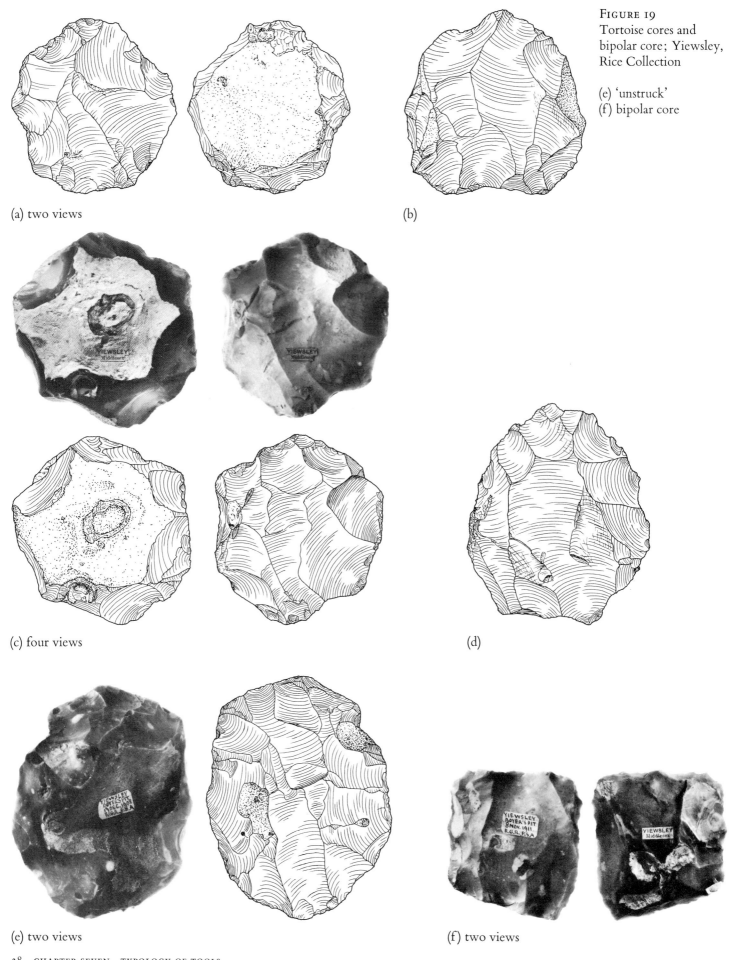

FIGURE 19
Tortoise cores and
bipolar core; Yiewsley,
Rice Collection

(e) 'unstruck'
(f) bipolar core

(a) two views

(b)

(c) four views

(d)

(e) two views

(f) two views

(a)

(b)

(c)

(d)

(e)

(f)

(g)

(h)

All stone tools are
reproduced at half size,
unless otherwise stated

FIGURE 21
Levallois flakes, longer
examples; Yiewsley,
Rice Collection

(a) 　　　　　　(b) 　　　　　　(c) 　　　　　　(d)

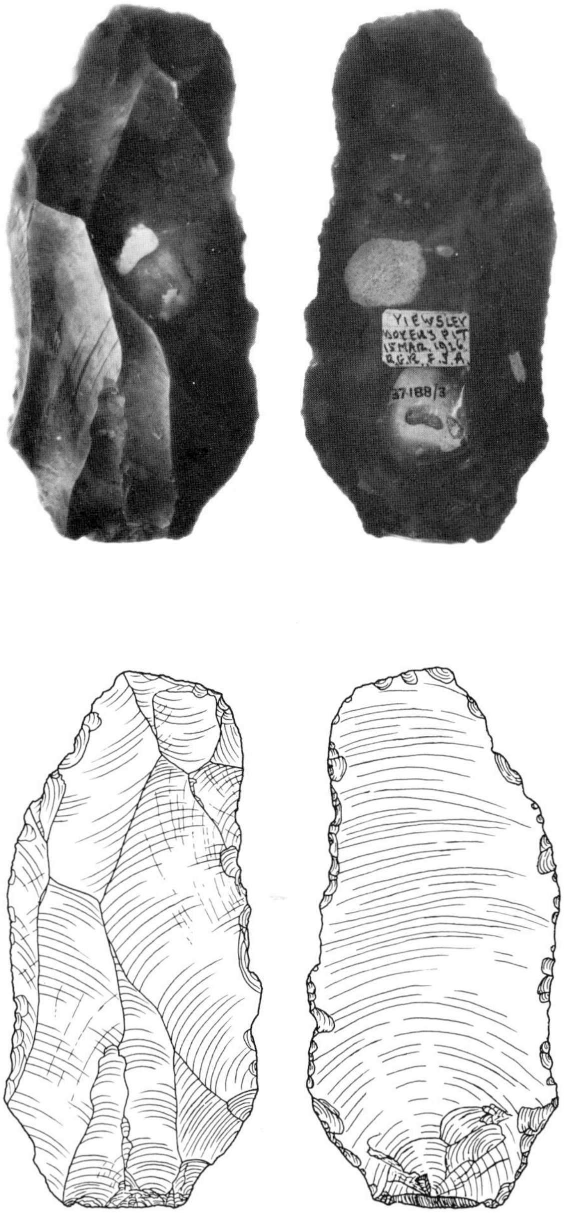

(e) four views

All stone tools are
reproduced at half size,
unless otherwise stated

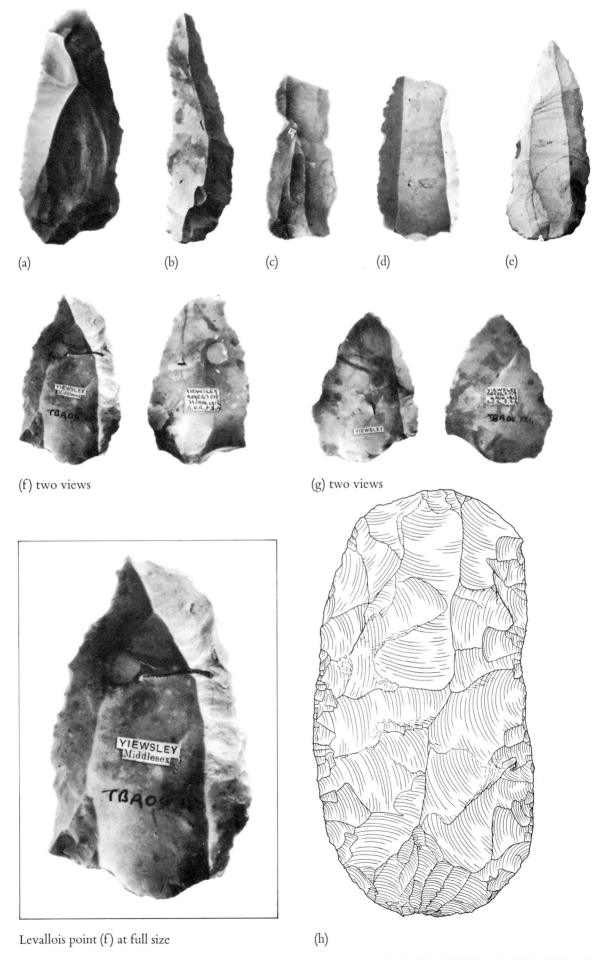

FIGURE 22
Levallois types;
Yiewsley, Rice
Collection

(a,b,c,d) Levallois blades
(e,f,g) Levallois points
(h) Retouched Levallois
flake (*British Museum*)

(a) (b) (c) (d) (e)

(f) two views (g) two views

Levallois point (f) at full size (h)

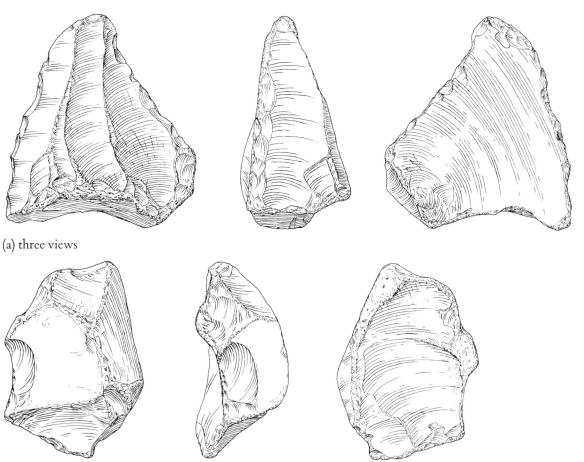

(a) three views

(b) three views

FIGURE 23
Clactonian flake and
core piece found north
of Warren Lake in 1972,
Yiewsley

(a) Clactonian flake
(b) core piece

All stone tools are
reproduced at half size,
unless otherwise stated

TABLE 5 Typology of the bluish-white series from Yiewsley (early Mousterian of Acheulian Tradition or Paxton stage) compared with le Tillet, Paxton, Oldbury and Kent's Cavern

	Yiewsley bluish-white series; Rice Collection	Yiewsley bluish-white series; Brown Collection	Yiewsley bluish-white series; Total	Le Tillet café-au-lait series [1]	Paxton Park pit, series AB [2]	Oldbury 'rock-shelter' [3]	Kent's Cavern level A2 [4]
Typical handaxes	5	7	12	15	8	44	5
Levallois points	3		3	12			
Levallois flakes	1	4	5	103	7	12	?
Tools (excluding handaxes)		2	2	67	1	26	13
Flakes and cores	2		2	91	200+	600+	28
Total	11	13	24	288	216+	682+	46
Analysis of handaxes							
'Pointed' HaP group	1		1	1	1	4	
HaP index			8.2	11.0	12.0	10.0	
Paxton type	1	2	3	3	3	6	1
Cordiform (MAT) group HaVc+Paxton	2	6	8	8	7	29	5
Cordiform group as percentage HaV			67	53	88	64	100
Cordiforms and long cordiforms HaV	3	7	10	10	7	31	5
Ovates HaLo	1		1	1		6	
Racloirs (included in tools)		2	2	29		16	7

1 Bordes, (1953).
2 Paterson and Tebbutt, (1947).
3 Collins and Collins, (1970).
4 Campbell and Sampson, (1971).

CHAPTER EIGHT

Stratigraphy of the Yiewsley palaeoliths

Regrettably, the great majority of palaeoliths from Yiewsley (and other sites) have never been recorded by layer. However some clues are available. The six handaxes found in Warren Lake (TQ 078 806) about 1955 are all known to come from the main fluviatile gravel (W1), and more probably from the lower than from the upper part. Interestingly, five of the six handaxes are typical pointed forms, which implies, in spite of the small size of the sample, an HaP index well over 50. The values for the main pits represented in the Rice Collection were, by contrast, below 50.

Further direct confirmation of artefacts in this gravel was provided by a small flake found in the 1972 section cleaning just south of the bluff at 2.2 m depth. It was in the Warrens gravel (W1) immediately underlying the Stockley solifluction gravel (W3).

The opening of Sabey's more recent pits, such as that close to Barnes Farm (TQ 082 808), has given us good exposures of a higher terrace (the Gouldsgreen terrace) north of the 125 ft (38 m) contour. From this terrace we have a typical Clactonian flake (figure 23), 2 less typical examples and 2 core pieces, one with a distinct Clactonian notch (figure 23). This latter and one of the flakes were found *in situ* in the Gouldsgreen gravel (G1); the others were almost certainly from the same deposit, but were surface finds.

On the west side of Stockley Road, the same terrace is present in the north-west pits (TQ 074 809) adjoining Chapel Lane. In the Lacaille Collection, in addition to some handaxes, there are some typical Clactonian flakes and cores marked 'Chapel Lane'. The handaxes may be presumed to come from the lower terrace. Brown seems to have found palaeoliths in 'Town pit', Hillingdon, on the Black Park or Boyn Hill terrace. But since it is unfortunately not known which artefacts were involved, or whether they came from fluviatile or post-fluviatile deposits, the discovery is almost without significance.

However, the most valuable evidence, in my opinion, has been overlooked for more than sixty years. Brown not only gave the best account of the strata of the canal pits, but also marked some 162 artefacts with their depth of discovery and occasionally with their stratum; these included 150 from Maynard's and Odell's (his Dawley pits) and 12 from Eastwood's and other pits he called 'West Drayton'. Because the stratigraphy seems to have been similar in each pit, and as the thickness of the layers are known, this evidence seems a most worthwhile clue.

The provenance of the bluish-white series seems reasonably clear (table 5). One of Rice's handaxes, now in the British Museum (no. 1933 4–6) is a whitish-grey cordiform, marked 'Broad's brickfield, Starveall, West Drayton, 1905, in clay 5 ft down'. The 'clay' obviously refers to the brickearth at the top of the sections.

A handaxe of Paxton type in the Brown Collection (no. 2193) was marked 'Eastwood's brickfield, West Drayton, in loam above gravel' (figure 24). A cordiform (no. 2821) was marked '3–5 ft down, just under the "uncallow" bleached layer, 1900'. No. 2167 of Paxton type but untypically subtriangular was marked '2½ ft from surface', and another cordiform was marked 'nearer surface'. Two racloirs were marked '4 and 5 ft' respectively, and a Levallois flake with a highly faceted butt was marked '3 ft'. All these tools clearly belong to the bluish-white series, and none were more than 6 ft (2 m) down.

FIGURE 24
Handaxes of Paxton type from whiteish series, Yiewsley

(a) Brown Collection
(*British Museum*)
Sturge 2193, marked 'in loam above gravel, Eastwoods Brickfield'

(b) Rice Collection

TABLE 6 Typology of those artefacts marked by J A Brown with their depth of recovery from Maynard's, Odell's, Eastwood's, Broad's and Pipkin's pits

Depths in feet as marked by Brown	Micoquian HaC	Lanceolate HaS	Ficron HaPf	Total 'pointed' group HaP	Long cordiforms HaVa	Short cordiforms HaVc	Other cordiforms HaVf	Total cordiform group HaV	Limandes Li	Ovates Lo	Others in the oval group HaLf	Total oval group HaL	Paxton type	Levallois flakes DL	Levallois cores CL	Racloirs R	Other flakes EF	Total artefacts
2–6													I					I
2½													I*					I*
3														I*				I*
4–5						3*		3*								2*		5*
6														3*				3*
7–8		½		½	1½+1*	1*		1½+2*	1			I						3+2*
9	1			I	1	1		2						2				5
10					2	1	1	4	1	1		2		2				8
11			1	I	1			I	1			I		2				5
12		½		½	2½	2		4½	1			I		I		I		8
13		1		I	3		2	5	1			I		3				10
14–15		4½	1	5½	12½	5		17½	1	1	1	3		I	2	I		30
16	3	5		8	9½	2	2½	14	2			2				I	I	24
17	1	5		6	6	1		7						I				14
18		4½		4½	½	1		1½	1			I		I				8
19–20†		14	1	16	12		1	13	1	1		2						31
below 20	1	1		2														2

* Bluish-white series.

½ Handaxes with one side convex and one side non-convex.

† Including black band

TABLE 7 Assemblages from pits at Yiewsley representing artefacts from the brickearth, the solifluction gravel and the fluviatile gravel (the latter divided into lower, middle and upper parts to produce assemblages of similar size)

Level	Micoquain HaC	Lanceolate HaS	Ficron HaPf	Total 'pointed' group HaP	Long cordiforms HaVa	Short cordifonrs HaVc	Other cordiforms HaVf	Total cordiform group HaV	Limandes Li	Ovates Lo	Others in the oval group HaLf	Total oval group HaL	Paxton type	Levallois flakes DL	Levallois cores CL	Racloirs R	Other flakes EF	Total artefacts and total handaxes
BW [1] 2–6 ft					1	4		5					2	4			2	13 Ha7
SXG [2] 7–12 ft		1	1	2	7	4	1	12	3	1		4		7		I		28 Ha20
UFG [3] 13–15 ft		5½	1	6½	15½	5	2	22½	2	1	1	4		4	2	I		40 Ha33
MFG [4] 16–17 ft	4	10		14	15½	3	2½	21	2			2		I		I	I	40 Ha37
LFG [5] 17 ft	2	19½	1	22½	12½	1	1	14½	2		1	3		I				41 Ha40

1 Brickearth and bluish-white series.

2 Solifluction 'unstratified' gravel, excluding two of bluish-white series.

3 Upper part of fluviatile (Warrens) gravel.

4 Middle part of fluviatile (Warrens) gravel.

5 Lower part of fluviatile (Warrens) gravel.

Three Levallois blades, all marked '6 ft' are of the buff colour, and two whitish handaxes were from '7 to 8 ft'. Two pieces in the Sadler Collection, an atypical handaxe and a Levallois flake with faceted butt, belong to the whitish series and are recorded as from '6 ft'. The bluish-white series is analysed in table 5. No pieces are known from more than 7 to 8 ft down. Similarly none of the very numerous artefacts with an iron-stained patina of brown or orange are from higher than 7 to 8 ft. This seems to be a thin overlap level. It is possible that the little-known buff series is a separate assemblage at about 6 ft down, but for the moment it seems safer to group it with the whitish series. As will be explained later, the whitish series belongs to the start of the Mousterian of Acheulian Tradition (MAT) or Paxton stage (Collins, 1969), and artefacts of the buff series could all belong in this stage, though they are more typical of the assemblage-type from Crayford (Collins, 1976). Brown gives the thickness of the brickearth or loam at the top of the section as 'about 5 ft', and accordingly it seems logical to attribute the whitish series to this loam, or possibly its base.

The artefacts in the Brown Collection with recorded depths have been classified by type and plotted according to their approximate depth in table 6. If these are grouped into 4 reasonably large assemblages below the whitish series (table 7), the results turn out to be remarkably consistent, both in terms of regular trends over time and in terms of similarity to the pattern found at Swanscombe (table 8). A first inspection suggested that pointed handaxes were more common in the lower levels and rare higher up, and the four groups consistently confirmed this. Such results suggest that Brown made few mistakes in recording the depth of the tools, and that the depth of the strata and their content of artefacts were indeed comparable in each pit. A twisted ovate marked '19 ft' may be wrongly ascribed, but this must be an exception. It should be remembered, however, that many pieces are marked as '14–15 ft' etc, and a few are recorded only as '15–18 ft'. No handaxe whose recorded depth is not precise to within 3 ft has been used in my sample. Where, for example, a range of '14–15 ft' is quoted I have used the deeper figure.

In grouping, the whitish series has first been separated off as the highest assemblage. The 28 artefacts with depths of 7 to 12 ft were grouped as probably representative of the assemblage from the solifluction gravel which is believed to include a Coombe rock. Artefacts from greater depths presumably represent the fluviatile Warrens gravel, and have been divided into three groups:

13–15 ft: the upper part (40 specimens);
16–17 ft: the middle part (40 specimens);
18 ft and below: the lower part (41 specimens).

TABLE 8 Comparison of apparent trends in data from the handaxe levels at Swanscombe and Yiewsley

Site	Pointed types HaP/Ha	Limandes HaLi/Ha	Levallois flakes DL/Ha+DL	Short cordiform HaVc/Ha	Suggested stages
Yiewsley	%	%	%	%	
BW Brickearth (bluish-white/whitish series) [1]	8.0	0.0	33.0	67.0	Paxton
SXG 'Unstratified' (Stockley) gravel	15.0	16.5	26.0	20.0	Northfleet I
UFG Upper part of Warrens gravel	19.6	6.2	10.8	15.0	?Cuxton II
MFG Middle part of Warrens gravel	37.9	5.4	2.7	8.0	Cuxton I
LFG Lower part of Warrens gravel	56.3	2.5	2.1	2.5	Barnfield II
Swanscombe					*Stages* [2]
Main Coombe rock [3]	15.4	21.0	90.0	no data	Northfleet I
Upper loam	25.9	30.0	20.0	no data	Cuxton II
Top of middle gravels	40.0	25.0	11.1	11.0	Cuxton I
Skull layer E	50.7	9.0	10.8	13.0	Barnfield II
Lower middle gravel	69.4	0.0	0.0	11.0	Barnfield I

1 Brown and Rice Collections.

2 Collins, 1969.

3 Based on a sample of 39 handaxes some of which may derive from earlier deposits.

The clearest trend in the five assemblages was the HaP index:

Lower fluviatile gravel (LFG): 56
Middle fluviatile gravel (MFG): 38
Upper fluviatile gravel (UFG): 20
Solifluction gravel (SXG): 15
Brickearth (whitish series): 8.

A major objective is to identify the level from which the majority of the Levallois flakes and cores in the iron-stained series originated. Here it must be pointed out that these are under-represented in the Brown series, compared with the Rice Collection. The Brown Collection has 19 Levallois flakes and 2 cores to 142 handaxes; the Rice Collection contains 388 Levallois flakes and 28 cores to 1229 handaxes. In Brown's depth-marked series, the number of Levallois types in the four groups was a follows: 1 (LFG); 1 (MFG); 6 (UFG); and 7 (SXG). This solifluction gravel, with 7 Levallois types to 20 handaxes, had nearly twice as many Levallois types proportionately to handaxes as the (UFG) level below, which had 6 Levallois types with 33 handaxes. We thus conclude that the solifluction gravel was the main Levallois level, and it remains an open question whether the upper part of the fluviatile gravel was really as rich in Levallois types, as is perfectly possible, or whether most of them have been wrongly attributed.

There are two published indications relevant to the level of the Levallois flakes. Brown (1895b, 163) noted 'a number of Palaeolithic implements of later age – long sharp spearheads, knives etc, have been discovered nearer the surface' (than the rest of the palaeoliths). 'These were generally 5 to 10 ft down, beneath the unstratified deposit'. The unstratified deposit is evidently the solifluction gravel, which Brown says was 5 to 12 ft down. This seems to tally best with a (?Levallois) level in or possibly at the base of the solifluction gravel. Marsden (1927, 297) said the Levallois flakes came from the top 8–9 ft of the section. This latter statement could of course refer to the whitish series.

Other trends are shown in table 8; some are similar to trends at Swanscombe (Collins, 1969 and 1976), but limandes (HaLi) are under-represented at Yiewsley compared with Swanscombe for reasons not fully understood at present. The culture implications of all the quantitative data set out here will be elaborated in the following sections.

CHAPTER NINE
Existing interpretations of the Palaeolithic

It is by no means self-evident what the aims of Palaeolithic research should be. Laymen often assume that we want above all to know what Palaeolithic 'tools' were used for. However, conclusive evidence on this point is virtually nonexistent. Even if we knew that a particular shape of tool was used for a particular purpose on one occasion, it would by no means follow that other tools of the same shape were used for the same purpose.

Much attention has been devoted to assigning evidence for Palaeolithic occupation to its correct geological, chronological and environmental context. The intention here is above all to answer the question 'How old is it?' The arrangement of the artefacts and assemblages in some kind of cultural scheme is another widely sought objective, and I believe that this is a fruitful study. But, whereas in the 1930s there was a great deal of optimism about producing a definitive culture scheme, the last decade has seen the reverse.

Breuil (1939) felt able to identify 7 Acheulian stages, 3 Clactonian stages and 7 Levalloisian stages. The confidence with which this scheme was applied slowly evaporated in the 1950s and 1960s. The belief that an expert, such as Breuil, could by intuition and experience arrange tools in the right order was belatedly questioned; and the fact that Breuil had never specified the precise criteria by which the stages were to be recognized became irrelevant when a new approach, based on the numerical characteristics of assemblages of associated artefacts, became normal in the 1960s.

Schemes of the earlier Palaeolithic are now held with less confidence and, fortunately, less dogmatism than for several decades. Leaving aside schemes which do not take account of the British evidence, Wymer, Waechter and the present writer are the main workers whose views are available in print. Wymer's scheme, although it has changed a little between 1961 and 1969, still comes close to being a mainstream view. It is to a large extent a distillation of generally held views, and it does not represent a radical break with pre-existing terminology, notably in using names like Middle Acheulian and Late Middle Acheulian which, as will be explained below, are roughly equivalent to the Barnfield and Cuxton stage in my scheme. Above all it represents a scheme based on some long-standing evidence from Swans-

combe. The evolution of these views is briefly reviewed below.

Hawkes, Oakley and Warren (of the Swanscombe Committee) discussed the problem carefully in 1938. They observed that a large sample of handaxes came from the middle gravels at Swanscombe. It included few ovate or cordiform handaxes. In the upper loam of that site, however, these types became frequent, along with the S–twist. The middle gravel's archaeological level was assigned to the Middle Acheulian 'culture'. The Swanscombe Committee (Hinton and others, 1938, 47) adopted the strange, even contradictory, view that the upper loam contained 'the beginnings of a more advanced phase of the Acheulian industry. But they do not take it outside the limits of our Middle Acheulian culture-stage as a whole'. Thus these authors pointed out the clear evidence for the two stages (their 'Middle Acheulian' and 'Late Middle Acheulian') most widely recognized by subsequent workers. However, they devalued this contribution by implying that the two really fundamental divisions were between the Early and Middle Acheulian on the one hand, and again the Middle and Late Acheulian on the other. So the two divisions they had recognized so clearly at Swanscombe (their 'Middle Acheulian' and 'Late Middle Acheulian') were implied to be not significantly different.

Previously, in 1926, Warren had recognized that twisted ovates belonged to a later stage than the 'typical' Acheulian; and Reginald Smith, in 1914, had taken a similar view. It seems that in the early years of the century this view was quite common; Sollas (1911) and Commont (several papers between 1908 and 1914) are examples. The terms used at this time were Chellian for the standard handaxe stage, St Acheul I for the twisted ovate stage, and St Acheul II for a more dubious pointed handaxe stage, immediately before the Mousterian. So the two stages 'Middle Acheulian' and 'Late Middle Acheulian' go back a long way in the history of Palaeolithic research, but they were almost always associated with ideas which are now regarded as dubious or unacceptable.

The suggestions of Wymer, Waechter and the present writer with their proposed culture stages, key sites or assemblages, dating and distinctive archaeological features are summarized in tables 9, 10 and 11.

TABLE 9 Palaeolithic sequence according to Wymer (1968)

Stage	Key sites and assemblages	Dating	Distinctive archaeological features
Levalloisian	Ebbsfleet upper loam Ponders End	Weichselian (Devensian)	
Levalloisian	Ebbsfleet lower gravel Crayford Acton Iver	Ipswichian	Levallois flakes
Acheulian (continued)	?Stoke Newington		
Deserted			
Levalloisian	Baker's Hole West Drayton	Late Wolstonian	Levallois flakes
Late Middle Acheulian	Swanscombe upper loam	Wolstonian formerly Gipping	Ovate-cordates S-twists Some Levallois flakes
Proto-Levalloisian	?Purfleet		Poor Levallois cores
Middle Acheulian	Swanscombe middle gravels Furze Platt Toots Farm	Later Hoxnian	Pointed handaxes predominate
Early Acheulian	?		
Clactonian	Swanscombe lower gravel Clacton	Early Hoxnian	Chopper-cores
?Early Acheulian	?	Anglian	

TABLE 10 Sequence of the Acheulian according to Waechter (1968)

Stages	Key sites and assemblages	Dating	Distinctive archaeological features
5 Mousterian of Acheulian Tradition	Erith Ipswich		Ovates
4 Acheulio-Levallois	Brundon St Neots Little Paxton ?Baker's Hole	Late Ipswichian	Ovates-Cordates, (thick-butted) Levallois flakes
3 Acheulio-Levallois	Yiewsley Farnham terrace C	Ipswichian	
2b Acheulian	Elveden	Late Hoxnian or Early Wolstonian	Ovates, sometimes twisted
2a Acheulian	Swanscombe upper loam		
1 Acheulian	Swanscombe middle gravels Furze Platt	Hoxnian	Lanceolate handaxes

Wymer's model (1968; 1961) is summarized in table 9. In terms of testability, this scheme would be easier to assess if rather more assemblages were quoted and the distinctive features expressed quantitatively. In terms of simplicity, the stages not based on well-dated assemblages (?Early Acheulian, Proto-Levalloisian and Late Acheulian) tend to complicate the scheme undesirably. In terms of omissions, the rather well-defined Early Mousterian of Acheulian Tradition (MAT) or Paxton stage does not figure;

and perhaps more support for the view that the Late Middle Acheulian spans two temperate periods and a cold phase should be offered. In terms of chronological testing, which will probably be the main form of testing for the foreseeable future, the following points of disagreement should be noted: Ebbsfleet upper loam (temperate bed) is not Weichselian; the Ebbsfleet lower gravel is not Ipswichian; and Stoke Newington is very unlikely on floral, faunal or altimetric grounds to be Ipswichian. But although

TABLE 11   Sequence of the Acheulian according to Collins[1]

Stage	Key sites and assemblages	Dating	Distinctive archaeological features
Paxton or early Mousterian of Acheulian Tradition MAT	Little Paxton Kent's Cavern Le Tillet 'café-au-lait' series	Early Weichselian or Devensian	Paxton handaxes Typical cordiforms
?Taubach	Ebbsfleet temperate bed	Late Ipswichian	Not very distinctive; some poor handaxes and denticulates
Crayfordian, probably not true Acheulian	Crayford Acton	Wolstonian-Ipswichian transition or early Ipswichian	Levallois points and blades 'Châpeau-de-gendarme' butts
Major break in British sequence			
Elveden	Elveden High Lodge Sands Westley ?Bowmans Lodge	Wolstonian interstadial	HaP 0–15 S-twist 15–50[3]
?Minor break			
Northfleet II	Ebbsfleet lower gravel	First main Wolstonian glacial stage	Bi-polar cores HaP 10–20 Levallois flakes over 50[2]
Northfleet I	Baker's Hole Bapchild New Hythe Montières	First main Wolstonian glacial stage	Tortoise cores HaP 10–20 Levallois cores over 50[2]
Cuxton II	Swanscombe upper loam Wansunt gravel St Acheul 'sables roux'	?Major 'interstadial' Proto-Wolstonian	HaP 10–25 S-twist 5–20[3] Levallois flakes 15–50[2]
Cuxton I	Swanscombe, top of middle gravels Cuxton Furze Platt Cagny 'presle'	Post-Hoxnian	HaP 25–50 Limandes over 20[3]
Barnfield II	Swanscombe skull level Dovercourt Stoke Newington 'floor'	Hoxnian IV	HaP 50–60
Barnfield I	Swanscombe lower middle gravels Stoke Newington 'gravels'	Hoxnian, late II and III	HaP index over 60 S-twist, limande and Levallois flakes all rare

1 Collins, 1969, 1970a, 1970b, and 1976;
Collins and Collins, 1970.

2 Percentage of sum of Levallois flakes and handaxes.

3 Percentage of typical handaxes.

some modifications seem desirable, Wymer's scheme has much to recommend it and deserves more attention.

Waechter (1968; 1970) offers for the Acheulian the model summarized in table 10. This scheme, although excellent in terms of simplicity, would be more readily testable if it included more assemblages for each stage and specified more characterization of the stages. Also some explanation seems necessary for the fact that nothing happens for most of the Wolstonian cold period. The significance of the flat-butted hand-axes of the Paxton stage seems to have been omitted. Chronological testing is possible, but can only be briefly touched on here. An Ipswichian date for Yiewsley seems unlikely, as also for Baker's Hole; the Levallois levels seem Wolstonian at latest. Little Paxton, on the other hand, seems to be Weichselian. As with Wymer's model, little provision is made for cultural or evolutionary testing, for example in the form of steadily changing indices.

The third model (table II), only the post-Clactonian part of which is given, comes from Collins (1966/70; 1969; 1970; and 1976; also Collins and Collins, 1970).

For simplicity a modification of this model could be made along the following lines. The Elveden stage could be merged with Cuxton II to produce the scheme Barnfield→Cuxton→Northfleet (?late Wolstonian)→Crayford (Ipswichian)→Paxton (early Devensian) as a continuous evolution. Although attractive in some ways, I feel this modification will not work; it is discussed at some length in Collins (1976). I would suggest that the scheme set out in table II is the most testable yet. It will surely need modification, and it is mainly up to others to test and criticize it. Nevertheless, I feel that we should urgently consider ways of increasing the testability of all the schemes.

We may now briefly consider how Wymer and Waechter have interpreted the Yiewsley sites. Wymer (1968,257) referred to ten feet of brick-earth with Levalloisian in or at its base overlying twenty feet of gravel with handaxes. The latter were usually rolled, and Wymer suggested (1968,270) that the high proportion of crude handaxes from West Drayton might indicate 'early Acheulian'. He also argues that the sheet of brickearth was laid down during the last interglacial by a high sea level of about 100 ft.

The view that the Levallois flakes are quite separate from the handaxes does not seem to square with the facts. The solifluction (Stockley) gravel, Brown's unstratified gravel, seems to have been the main Levallois level and also to have been a rich handaxe level; likewise the brickearth over it had Levallois flakes and handaxes, the latter Mousterian in type. My analysis did not offer any support for an Early Acheulian in the Lynch Hill terrace or any higher terrace. We have demonstrated that there are at least two loams or brickearths, neither seem to be last interglacial, and there really is no reason at present to associate their deposition with a high sea or river level, but this question is being further investigated.

Waechter (1970,17) thought the Rice Collection was from an 'Upper Taplow' terrace and consisted of four series:

a. slightly rolled Clactonian flakes;
b. slightly rolled Middle Acheulian handaxes derived from the Boyn Hill terrace further north;
c. unrolled handaxes of later date than the Swanscombe middle gravel and upper loam, resembling the north French Acheulian of the end of the last interglacial;
d. unrolled typical Levallois types like Crayford, Ebbsfleet and Acton.

Some rolled Levallois flakes make a possible fifth series. All these artefacts are regarded as coming from the terrace gravel, and none from the overlying solifluction and loam. The terrace is dated to the last interglacial.

Waechter's view that no Yiewsley artefacts came from above the terrace gravel cannot be correct, for both the loam with its white series and the solifluction gravel yielded implements. The Clactonian flakes, however, may well derive from the terrace above (the Gouldsgreen gravel). The view that the Boyn Hill terrace (*sensu stricto*) is a main handaxe-bearing terrace is highly questionable (Collins, 1976). Instead it is regularly the Lynch Hill terrace which contains the 'typical Acheulian' (Barnfield and Cuxton stages). The evolution of the handaxe typology of this terrace at Yiewsley does not suggest that it contains much derived Acheulian.

Neither the unrolled handaxes nor those from higher levels at Yiewsley seem to resemble the 'Late Acheulian' of northern France; but the whitish series certainly resembles the early Mousterian of Acheulian Tradition (MAT) at sites like le Tillet. The Levallois element (especially the tortoise cores and Levallois ovates) is not very like Crayford or Acton, for in the Crayfordian tortoise cores are absent and the characteristic features are Levallois points, Levallois blades and 'châpeau-de-gendarme' butts. The buff-coloured series from Yiewsley, however, may represent a Crayfordian.

CHAPTER TEN

Some suggestions concerning the interpretation of the Yiewsley Palaeolithic

The archaeological sequence at Yiewsley seems to be as follows:

a. Gouldsgreen gravel (G1): ?Clactonian;
b. Warrens gravel (W1) (lower, middle and upper parts): Acheulian, Barnfield and Cuxton stages;
c. Warrens loam, base of Stockley gravel and Stockley gravel (W2 and 3): Acheulian, ?late Cuxton and Northfleet stages;
d. Stockley loam (W4): ?Crayford and Paxton stages.

With only 5 artefacts from the Gouldsgreen gravel, and about a dozen from its equivalent in the Chapel Lane pits, further confirmation is needed of a Clactonian stage. But what cannot reasonably be doubted is that this gravel is implementiferous and has traces of fire. So it seems that we are not dealing with a geological deposit earlier than the arrival of man in this part of the Thames basin. It is normal for Clactonian to precede the Barnfield stage of the Acheulian, notably at Swanscombe, but also at Britwell near Farnham, Buckinghamshire, at Stoke Newington (Collins, 1976 Campbell excavations), at Barnham, Suffolk and probably at Ipswich, Suffolk. If the Gouldsgreen gravel continues downstream into the lower gravels at Swanscombe, then it will be the Rickson stage of the Clactonian which is involved.

Brown's finds from 18 ft or more in the lower part of the Warrens gravel (LFG), seem to equate with the assemblage from the lower part of the Swanscombe upper middle gravel (skull level); the HaP index of 56.3 on 40 handaxes is a little higher than the 50.7 for Swanscombe and close to Dovercourt with 54.7. I have called this stage Barnfield II. The middle part of the Warrens gravel, (Brown's 16 and 17 ft series) (MFG), has an HaP index of 37.9. This is a little lower than the index for the top of the Swanscombe upper middle gravel (40.0) or for Cuxton itself (43.0), but is very close to the figure for the 'presle' at Cagny (37.8). These are grouped as Cuxton I stage.

Brown's 13 to 15 ft series (UFG), which may in reality come from the surface of the Warrens gravel or be contemporary with the Warrens loam, has an HaP index of 19.6. This is a little lower than the estimate for the Swanscombe upper loam, and compares well with the values for assemblages from the Amiens region which overlie the presle; the Cagny shell loam (about 16); and the famous 'Atelier Commont' from the 'sables roux' of St Acheul (17.5). These are grouped as Cuxton II; but the

Yiewsley series could also be a mixture of an earlier Cuxton stage and a Northfleet stage.

From the Stockley gravel or its base (Brown's 7 to 12 ft series) the handaxes have an HaP index of about 15; this is probably the main Levallois flake and tortoise core level. This is equated with the Baker's Hole main Coombe rock assemblage. Levallois flakes dominate at Baker's Hole, but are in a minority in the small series of 28 artefacts marked by Brown. In the large Rice Collection Levallois flakes were about as numerous as handaxes, although this collection obviously includes artefacts from some levels with almost no Levallois flakes; thus, in reality, Levallois flakes were almost certainly dominant in the Stockley gravel. This stage of the Acheulian is referred to as Northfleet I. (In the past this has often been referred to as Levalloisian).

The Stockley loam may be separated from the underlying gravel by a long erosional period, and the latter seems to be heavily weathered. The whitish assemblage from this loam may be compared with the following assemblages: Little Paxton; le Tillet 'café-au-lait' series; Kent's Cavern A2; Bramford Road, Ipswich; Christchurch, Bournemouth; Erith foreshore; Ham Hill, Snodland, Kent; and Marlow brickyard in Buckinghamshire. This stage has been called the Paxton stage of the Acheulian or Mousterian of Acheulian Tradition (MAT). Most of the sites are believed to belong to the early part of the last glaciation.

Interestingly, this level seems to include true Levallois points, as le Tillet, for example, but these are more typical of the Crayfordian. It remains an open question whether a Crayfordian is represented at Yiewsley by, for example, the three Levallois blades of the buff series at 6 ft in the Brown measured series. Such an assemblage might lie stratigraphically on the Stockley gravel surface. But most of the Levallois flakes, even some with 'châpeau-de-gendarme' butts, could belong with the Northfleet assemblage, and other late Levallois types seem to go with the Paxton stage.

CHAPTER ELEVEN

Prospects and desirability of future research

Further gravel digging on the Gouldsgreen (higher) terrace is taking place at present, and this should be watched for palaeoliths. There may, from time to time, be exposures on the main (Lynch Hill) terrace, and any records of palaeoliths *in situ* would be valuable. Large assemblages are, however, unlikely to turn up. It is hoped to put down one or more boreholes near Warren Lake, to fix more accurately the level of the London clay bench, and to take samples for pollen analysis through the Warrens gravel.

Re-exposure of the strata close to the canal would be most valuable, and some localities still have brickearth, with no doubt the lower strata, remaining. As part of a long-term programme of research, a series of such sections should be examined geologically and palaeobiologically for any clues to the refinement of the sequence of events known so far. In this way it should also be possible to test some of the theories advanced here.

Exposures at present available will, it is hoped, be studied soon, notably at Boyer's fishing lake and the brickearths at Iver. It is important to see if they are contemporary with the deposits already investigated and more generally to date the brickearth spreads.

A realistic objective would be the mapping of the benches on which the West Middlesex terraces lie. This could be done from new exposures, or partly from existing borehole records. All this work should perhaps best be seen as part of a much-needed long term study of the Thames Pleistocene and Palaeolithic, as proposed in the survey of the archaeology of the London area currently being prepared by the London and Middlesex Archaeological Society (Collins, 1976).

BIBLIOGRAPHY

BASTIN, B and CoÛTEAUX, M. 1966. Application de la méthode de Frenzel à l'extraction des pollens dans les sédiments archéologiques pauvres. *L'Anthropologie*, Vol. 70, 201–203.

BORDES, F. 1953. Les limons quaternaires de la bassin de la Seine. (Masson).

— 1961. Typologie du Paléolithique ancien et moyen. (Delmas).

BREUIL, H. 1939. The Pleistocene succession in the Somme valley. *Proceedings of the Prehistoric Society*, Vol. 5, 33–38.

BROMEHEAD, C E N. 1912. On the diversion of a bourne near Chertsey. *Geological Survey Summary of Progress for 1911*.

BROWN, J A. 1886. The Thames valley surface deposits of the Ealing district and their associated Palaeolithic floors. *Quarterly Journal of the Geological Society*, Vol. 42, 192–200.

— 1887. *Palaeolithic man in north-west Middlesex*. (Macmillan).

— 1888. On the discovery of Elephas Primigenius associated with flint implements at Southall. *Proceedings of the Geologists' Association*, Vol. 10, 361–372.

— 1895a (sometimes given as 1896). Excursion to Hanwell, Dawley and West Drayton. *Proceedings of the Geologists' Association*, Vol. 14, 118–120.

— 1895b (sometimes given as 1896). Notes on the high level drift between Hanwell and Iver. *Proceedings of the Geologists' Association*, Vol. 14, 153–173.

CALLOW, W J, BAKER, M J and PRITCHARD, DAPHNE M. 1964. National Physical Laboratory radiocarbon measurements II. *Radiocarbon*, Vol. 6, 25–30.

— — and HASSALL, GERALDINE I. 1966. National Physical Laboratory radiocarbon measurements IV. *Radiocarbon*, Vol. 8, 340–347.

CAMPBELL, JOHN B and SAMPSON, C G. 1971. A new analysis of Kent's Cavern, Devonshire, England. *University of Oregon Anthropological Papers*, No. 3.

COLLINS, DESMOND. 1969. Culture traditions and environment of early man. *Current Anthropology*, Vol. 10, 267–316.

— 1970a. Stone artefact analysis and recognition of culture traditions. *World Archaeology*, Vol. 2, 17–27.

— 1970b. The recognition of traditions and phases in culture from quantitative studies of stone technology. *Actes du VIIe Congrès International des Sciences Préhistoriques et Protohistoriques, 1966.* (Prague: Institute of Archaeology ČSAV).

— 1971. Palaeolithic renaissance. (Discussion of recent excavations at Swanscombe, Northfleet and Clacton). *The London Archaeologist*, Vol. I, ii, 259–260.

— 1976. Palaeolithic and Mesolithic. *In* The Archaeology of the London area: current knowledge and problems. *London and Middlesex Archaeological Society Special Paper No. 1.*

COLLINS, DESMOND and ANN. 1970. Excavations at Oldbury in Kent; cultural evidence for last glacial occupation in Britain. *Bulletin of the Institute of Archaeology*, Vols. 8 and 9, 151–176.

COMMONT, V. 1908. Les industries de l'ancien St Acheul. *L'Anthropologie*, Vol. 19, 257.

CULLING, E W H. 1956. Longitudinal profiles of the Chiltern streams. *Proceedings of the Geologists' Association*, Vol. 67, 314–345.

DEWEY, H and BROMEHEAD, C E N. 1922. The geology of south London. *Memoir of the Geological Survey. Explanation of sheet 270.*

DIMBLEBY, G W. 1957. The pollen analysis of terrestrial soils. *New Phytologist*, Vol. 56, 12–28.

ERD, K. 1970. Pollen-analytical classification of the Middle Pleistocene in the German Democratic Republic. *Palaeogeography, Palaeoclimatology, Palaeoecology*, Vol. 8, 129–145.

— and ČEPEK, A. 1969. Pollenstratigraphie vom Holstein-Interglazial bis zum Frühweichsel Glazial in der DDR. *VIIIe Congrès INQUA: Resumé des communications*, Vols. 84 and 196. (Paris).

EVANS, P. 1971. The Phanerozoic time-scale. A supplement (part 2): Towards a Pleistocene time-scale. *Geological Society Special Publication*, Vol. 5.

FRANKS, J W. 1960. Interglacial deposits at Trafalgar Square. *New Phytologist*, Vol. 59, 145–152.

FRENZEL, B. 1964. Zur Pollenanalyse von Lössen. *Eiszeitalter und Gegenwart*, Vol. 15, 5–39.

GODWIN, H. 1958. Pollen analysis in mineral soil. An interpretation of a podzol pollen analysis by Dr G W Dimbleby. *Flora*, Vol. 146, 321–327.

GUILLET, B and PLANCHAIS, N. 1969. Note sur une technique d'extraction des pollens des sols par une solution dense. *Pollen et spores*, Vol. 11, 141–145.

HARE, F K. 1947. The geomorphology of a part of the middle Thames. *Proceedings of the Geologists' Association*, Vol. 58, 294–339.

HAVINGA, A J. 1971. An experimental investigation into the decay of pollen and spores in various soil types. Pp 446–479. *In* BROOKES, J and others (editors). *Sporopollenin*. (Academic Press).

HINTON, M A C and KENNARD, A S. 1906. The relative ages of the stone implements of the lower Thames valley. *Proceedings of the Geologists' Association*, Vol. 19, 76–100.

JUKES-BROWNE, A J and WHITE, H J O. 1908. The geology of the country around Henley-on-Thames and Wallingford. *Memoir of the Geological Survey. Explanation of sheet 254.*

KELLY, M R. 1968. Floras of Middle and Upper Pleistocene age from Brandon, Warwickshire. *Philosophical Transactions of the Royal Society*, B, Vol. 254, 401.

KING, W B R and OAKLEY, K P. 1936. The Pleistocene succession in the lower part of the Thames valley. *Proceedings of the Prehistoric Society*, Vol. 2, 52–76.

LACAILLE, A D. 1938. A Levallois side-scraper from the brickearth at Yiewsley. *Antiquaries Journal*, Vol. 18, 55–57.

LEESON, J R and LAFFAN, G B. 1894. On the geology of the Pleistocene deposits in the valley of the Thames at Twickenham. *Quarterly Journal of the Geologists' Association*, Vol. 50, 453–462.

LUTTIG, G. 1968. Ansichten, Bestrebungen und Beschlüsse der Subkommission for Europäische Quartärstratigraphie der INQUA (SEQS 2). *Eiszeitalter und Gegenwart*, Vol. 19, 233–238.

MARSDEN, J G. 1928. Notes on le Moustier flints from Acton, West Drayton and Iver. *Proceedings of the Prehistoric Society of East Anglia*, Vol. 5, 297–298.

MENKE, B. 1968. Beiträge zur Biostratigraphie des Mittelpleistozäns in Norddeutschland. *Meyniana*, Vol. 18, 35–42.

MITCHELL, G F, PENNY, L F, SHOTTON, F W and WEST, R G. 1973. A correlation of Quaternary deposits in the British Isles. *Geological Society of London Special Report*, Vol. 4, 99.

OVEY, C D (editor). 1964. The Swanscombe skull. *Royal Anthropological Institute Occasional Paper*, Vol. 20.

PATERSON, T T and TEBBUTT, C F. 1947. Palaeoliths from St Neots, Huntingdonshire. *Proceedings of the Prehistoric Society*, Vol. 13, 37–46.

POCOCK, T I. 1903. Summary of progress for 1902. *Geological Survey U.K.*, Vol. 199.

ROE, DEREK A. 1968. A gazetteer of the British Lower and Middle Palaeolithic sites. *CBA Research Report*, Vol. 8.

ROSS, B R M. 1932a. The physiographic evolution of the Kennet-Thames. *British Association Report*, 1931, 368.

— 1932b. A contribution to the study of the geomorphology and drainage development of the lower Thames basin. (University of London D. Phil. thesis).

ROWLEY, J R and WALCH, K M. 1972. Recovery of introduced pollen from a mountain glacier stream. *Grana*, Vol. 12, 146–152.

SANER, B R M and WOOLDRIDGE, S W. 1929. River development in Essex. *Essex Naturalist*, Vol. 21, 244–250.

SEALY, K R. 1964. Land use on the Thames terraces and adjoining country in west Middlesex and Buckinghamshire. *20th International Geographical Congress: Guide to London excursions*, 83–87.

— and SEALY, CATHERINE E. 1956. The terraces of the middle Thames. *Proceedings of the Geologists' Association*, Vol. 67, 369–392.

SHERLOCK, R L. 1924. On the superficial deposits of south Herts and south Bucks. *Proceedings of the Geologists' Association*, Vol. 35, 19–28.

— and NOBLE, A N. 1912. On the glacial origin of the clay-with-flints of Buckinghamshire and on a former course of the Thames. *Quarterly Journal of the Geological Society*, Vol. 68, 199–212.

SHOTTON, F W and WILLIAMS, R E G. 1973. Birmingham University radiocarbon dates VII. *Radiocarbon*, Vol. 15, 451–468.

SIMPSON, I M and WEST, R G. 1957. On the stratigraphy and palaeobotany of a late Pleistocene organic deposit at Chelford, Cheshire. *New Phytologist*, Vol. 57, 239–250.

SMITH, R A and DEWEY, H. 1914. The high terrace of the Thames. *Archaeologia*, Vol. 65, 187–212.

— 1931. *The Sturge Collection*, Vol. 1. (The British Museum).

SOLLAS, W J. 1911. *Ancient hunters*. (Macmillan).

SPARKS, B W and others. 1969. Hoxnian interglacial deposits near Hatfield. *Proceedings of the Geologists' Association*, Vol. 80, 243–267.

SUTCLIFFE, A J. 1964. The mammalian fauna. Pp 85–111. *In* OVEY, C D (editor). *The Swanscombe Skull*. (Royal Anthropological Institute).

SWANSCOMBE COMMITTEE. (chairman: M A C Hinton). 1938. Report on the Swanscombe skull. *Journal of the Royal Anthropological Institute*, Vol. 68, 17–98.

THOMAS, M F. 1961. River terraces and drainage development in the Reading area. *Proceedings of the Geologists' Association*, Vol. 72, 415–436.

TRATMAN, E K, DONOVAN, D T and CAMPBELL, J B. 1971. The Hyaena den (Wookey Hole), Mendip Hills, Somerset. *Proceedings of the University of Bristol Spelaeological Society*, Vol. 12, 245.

TREACHER, L I and WHITE, H J O. 1909. Excursion to Maidenhead. *Proceedings of the Geologists' Association*, Vol. 21, 198–201.

TURNER, C. 1970. The Middle Pleistocene deposits at Marks Tey, Essex. *Philosophical Transactions of the Royal Society*, Vol. 257, 373–440.

VULLIAMY, C E. 1930. *The archaeology of London and Middlesex*. (Methuen).

WAECHTER, J D. 1968. The evidence of the Levallois technique in the British Acheulian. In *La Préhistoire*. (Paris: CNRS).

— 1970. The Lower Palaeolithic age. Pp 11–20. In *Victoria County History. Middlesex*, Vol. 1.

WARREN, S H. 1926. The classification of the Lower Palaeolithic with special reference to Essex. *Transactions of the SE Union of Scientific Studies*, 38–40.

WEST, R G. 1968. *Pleistocene geology and biology*. (Longmans).

— and others. 1964. Interglacial deposits at Ilford, Essex. *Philosophical Transactions of the Royal Society*, Vol. 247, 185–212.

WHITAKER, W. 1889. The geology of London and of parts of the Thames valley. *Memoir of the Geological Survey*, Vol. 1.

WHITE, H J O. 1895. On the distribution and relations of the Westleton and glacial gravels in parts of Oxfordshire and Berkshire. *Proceedings of the Geologists' Association*, Vol. 14, 11–30.

WOOLDRIDGE, S W. 1938. The glaciation of the London basin, and the evolution of the lower Thames drainage system. *Quarterly Journal of the Geological Society*, Vol. 94, 627–667.

— and LINTON, D L. 1939. 1955. 2nd Ed. *Structure, surface and drainage in south-east England*. (Geo. Philip and Son Ltd).

WRIGHT, W B. 1937. The Quaternary Ice Age. (Macmillan).

WYMER, JOHN. 1961. The Lower Palaeolithic succession in the Thames valley. *Proceedings of the Prehistoric Society*, Vol. 27, 1–27.

— 1968. *Lower Palaeolithic archaeology in Britain*. (Baker).

ZAGWIJN, W H, MONTFRANS, H M van and ZANDSTRA, J G. 1971. Subdivision of the Cromerian in the Netherlands: pollenanalysis, palaeomagnetism and sedimentary petrology. *Geologie in Mijnbouw*, Vol. 50, 41–58.

ZEUNER, F E. 1945. *The Pleistocene period*. (The Ray Society).

HER MAJESTY'S STATIONERY OFFICE

Government Bookshops

49 High Holborn, London WC1V 6HB
13a Castle Street, Edinburgh EH2 3AR
41 The Hayes, Cardiff CF1 1JW
Brazennose Street, Manchester M60 8AS
Southey House, Wine Street, Bristol BS1 2BQ
258 Broad Street, Birmingham B1 2HE
80 Chichester Street, Belfast BT1 4JY

Government publications are also available through booksellers

The full range of Museum publications is displayed and
sold at the Museum of London
Obtainable in the United States of America from
Pendragon House Inc., 2595 East Bayshore Road,
Palo Alto, California 94303

Two major archaeological reports are being published by
the Museum of London: *Early Man in West Middlesex* and
2000 years of Brentford. They celebrate the transfer of the
former London Museum from Kensington Palace to the
new site in the City where it has been joined with the
former Guildhall Museum. They also represent the
triumphant conclusion to a rich period of archaeological
research undertaken by or on behalf of the London
Museum.

In June 1975 the London Museum, together with the
Guildhall Museum, its sister institution in the City, was
vested in the splendid Museum of London housed in
purpose-built premises in the Barbican. Both in the City
and in Greater London, the new institution is continuing
and extending the archaeological contribution of its
precursors.

Printed in England for Her Majesty's Stationery Office by
Raithby, Lawrence & Company Limited at the De Montfort Press:
Leicester and London
Dd 29688 K16